TIME IS A TOY

BY MICHAEL BENEDIKT

POEMS

Changes: A Chapbook, New Fresco (Detroit), 1961
The Body, Wesleyan University Press (Middletown, Conn.), 1968
Sky, Wesleyan University Press, 1970
Mole Notes, Wesleyan University Press, 1971
Night Cries, Wesleyan University Press, 1976
The Badminton at Great Barrington; or, Gustav Mahler & the Chattanooga Choo-Choo, University of Pittsburgh Press, 1980

PLAYS

The Vaseline Photographer, first produced in New York City, 1965
Box, first produced in New York City, 1970

EDITED COLLECTIONS

(With George E. Wellwarth) *Modern French Theatre: The Avant-Garde, Dada, and Surrealism*, Dutton, 1964
(With George E. Wellwarth) *Postwar German Theatre: An Anthology of Plays*, Dutton, 1967
(And translator) *Ring Around the World: The Selected Poems of Jean L'Anselme*, Rapp & Whiting, 1967, Swallow Press, 1968
Theatre Experiment: New American Plays, Doubleday, 1967
(With George E. Wellwarth) *Modern Spanish Theatre: An Anthology of Plays*, Dutton, 1968
(And translator) *22 Poems of Robert Desnos*, Kayak, 1971
(And translator) *The Poetry of Surrealism: An Anthology*, Little, Brown, 1974
(And co-translator) *The Prose Poem: An International Anthology*, Dell, 1976

TIME IS A TOY

The Selected Poems of Michael Benedikt

Edited by John Gallaher & Laura Boss

The University of Akron Press
Akron, Ohio

18 17 16 15 14 5 4 3 2 1

ISBN: 978-1-937378-79-0 (paper)
ISBN: 978-1-629220-06-2 (ePDF)
ISBN: 978-1-629220-07-9 (ePub)

LIBRARY OF CONGRESS CATALOGING-IN-PUBLICATION DATA
Benedikt, Michael, 1935–2007.
[Poems. Selections]
Time Is a Toy : The Selected Poems of Michael Benedikt / Michael Benedikt ; Edited by John Gallaher & Laura Boss. — First Edition.
pages cm Includes bibliographical references.
ISBN 978-1-937378-79-0 (paperback : alk. paper)
I. Gallaher, John, 1965– II. Boss, Laura, 1938– III. Title.
PS3552.E54A6 2013 811'.54—dc23
2013034032

∞ The paper used in this publication meets the minimum requirements of ANSI/NISO z39.48–1992 (Permanence of Paper).

Cover design: Lauren McAndrews

Time is a Toy was designed and typeset in Stone Print with Futura display by Amy Freels, with assistance from Lauren McAndrews, and printed on sixty-pound natural and bound by Bookmasters of Ashland, Ohio.

CONTENTS

*Revised by Michael Benedict after original book publication

THE BENEDIKT SUITCASE

John Gallaher

I graduated high school in 1983, and by that time had already started collecting anthologies and all the inexpensive and free books I could. Several of the anthologies I had (*Contemporary American Poets,* edited by Donald Hall; *The Young American Poets*, edited by Paul Carroll; *The Major Young Poets*, edited by Al Lee, etc.) included work from Michael Benedikt, who also was the editor of two anthologies that were fundamentally important to me (and many others I've talked with over the years): *The Poetry of Surrealism* and *The Prose Poem: An International Anthology*. As time went on, and I found more and more anthologies and books, I lost track of Benedikt, only to discover him again a couple years ago as I was moving my office and came across my stash of poetry anthologies from the 1970s. Not to lose him again, I went looking for more of his work, only to find he had died a few years earlier and had published no more books after 1980, and what he had published was long out of print.

With help and encouragement from Don Share, I was able to get in touch with Laura Boss, who owns the rights to his work and had saved his archives from going to a dumpster. She quickly signed on to bringing Benedikt's work back into print, thus beginning what has become the wonderful, if amazingly time-consuming, project of putting this book together.

Michael Benedikt never stopped revising his work, even after publication. For the work selected from his five published books, I've made the decision to stick to the versions from those books, with a few exceptions (which are noted in the table of contents), though the grammar of some poems has been edited for consistency. For his unpublished books, I've stuck as closely as I could to what seemed to be the final versions of the manuscript before he moved on to other work, though sometimes those lines blurred (especially in the later work of *Transitions* and *OF:*).

The difficulty in working with Benedikt's unpublished work is that various drafts of many of his poems exist, sometimes dated, sometimes not, and his editing notes are often in faint pencil on yellowed or poorly photocopied paper. Also, he would often retype sections and paste them over the older versions, but, over time, some of these pasted-on sections have fallen off. From what I've been able to find, what follows, then, is as close to what would have been his chronological publication history, if he had published the work he intended to publish, when he completed (or abandoned) it.

While Benedikt was writing his first two published books, *The Body* (1968) and *Sky* (1970), he was also writing the prose poems of *Universe*. It appears that an early version of *The Body* included a number of these prose poems, but, on Robert Bly's advice, Benedikt excluded them from the final version of either of those books. After the publication of *Mole Notes* (1971), Benedikt was sending *Universe* out to potential publishers, as well as *Night Cries*, which ended up being his fourth book published, in 1976, leaving *Universe* unpublished (which he never attempted to publish again). By that time, he also had another manuscript of prose poems, *Persephone's Telephone*, that he continued to work on (as far as I can tell) for another couple of years without ever seeking a publisher.

In the mid-70s, Benedikt was exceptionally prolific. As an author, he had published four books in eight years, while also editing two large anthologies (on Surrealism and the prose poem that I mentioned earlier), serving as poetry editor of *The Paris Review* (1975–78), and teaching at Boston University (1977–80). As busy as this time was for him professionally, it was difficult for him personally. All his life he had difficulty leaving the house, and change was difficult for him. His divorce in 1977 was, therefore, quite traumatic for him, as was his move (at the same time) to Boston after a lifetime in New York.

Also during this time, Benedikt had a folder he was calling "Puffton Poems (Poems from Amherst)," which appears to be where he was keeping poems he was working on, and it's unclear if he ever intended it as a proper manuscript (though many of the poems in it were published in journals and anthologies at the time). It's in this folder that the first version of "OF POETRY, MY FRIEND" appears, though he continued to go back and work on it, in 1997 and then again in 2007, but possibly other times as well. Some of the poems from this folder/manuscript were published in *Benedikt: A Profile* (1977).

Benedikt had *The Badminton at Great Barrington* largely drafted by 1977, and he had also begun writing what was intended to be a two-volume work titled *Family Blessings / Family Curses*, which consumed him for the next ten years, and was the beginning of his obsessive revising and inability to finish poems (and manuscripts), which kept him from ever seriously seeking book publication again. The first volume, subtitled "Departures & Arrivals"—which was to be a chronicle of his time in Boston, while dealing with his divorce, teaching at Boston University, and attempting to establish new relationships, as well as his life with, and the death of, his cat—was finally completed in 1988. Because of the length of these poems (he called them his "little epics"), I've had to excerpt from two of them, due to space limitations, while including the full text of three others, to present something of its general arc. The projected book contained fourteen poems, along with a lengthy prose preface. The poems included in this volume ("LIKE MANY OTHER NECESSARILY PERIPATETIC AMERICANS . . .", "FOR GERALD FENICHEL . . .", "TO PEGGY GABSON . . .", "DON HALL & JANE KENYON . . .", and "XMAS ON BAY STATE ROAD . . .") are poems one, four, five, eleven, and fourteen.

There are mentions of a second volume in his foreword to *Family Blessings / Family Curses*, and at one point he seems to be indicating that this second volume is either written or drafted, but no such volume exists with that name, though, from indications of its contents, it appears that Benedikt's next manuscript, *Transitions*, is (at least to some extent) a version of what the second volume was to have included (including the poem "OF FRIENDSHIP VS. CONFLICT OF INTEREST . . ." which he later included with his poems for *OF:)*. *Transitions* seems to have been more abandoned than completed, sometime around the middle of the 1990s, when Benedikt moved away from writing about his personal history to writing the more subject-oriented poems of *OF:*, which he continued to draft and work on until the time of his death in 2007, including the incomplete "OF GARTER BELTS . . ." that he was working on mostly from 1988 to 1992, and which I've pieced together from various drafts to include here.

Finally, the poem "TIME," which closes this book, was published in the June 1964 issue of *Poetry*, and never included in a book or a manuscript folder. Benedikt mentioned the poem in an interview included in *Benedikt: A Profile*, saying it was going to be included in an anthology (though I could find no verification if that happened). At that time he also said that, along with "TIME," there were dozens of other poems from the '60s that he intended to collect at some point. I've decided to include this poem as an afterword to stand for these uncollected, and mostly lost, poems.

There were hints throughout the '70s that Michael Benedikt might disappear from 'the poetry scene.' He admitted a great sympathy of shared subterranean endeavor with his character of Mole from *Mole Notes*, for instance, and in his 1968 note in *The Young American Poets* anthology, writes: "A condition in which all possibilities are open, offering the widest range of choice, including the choice of not choosing at all—not writing, I mean—strikes me as a real spiritual condition. . . . I want my own poetry, increasingly, to contain a maximum of spiritual information" (87). A decade later he echoed this again in an interview published in *Benedikt: A Profile*: "It's essential to the writing experience that I have to not write; and not to worry about it, either. I've learned after all these years that my mind is moving on, doing what it can, even in the absence of my pencil" (25–26). And if not for the actions of Laura Boss, to save as many poems as she could find after his death, more than half of the poems in this volume would be lost forever.

As well, this book wouldn't be possible if it weren't for the help and encouragement of many people, including Don Share and Robert Archambeau, and without those who helped me get the poems typed out: Teresa Cole, Karlee Liberty, Emily Reeb, Samantha Wood, John Wallace, Riley Bean, and Michelle Barbieri. Miles and miles of thanks to my co-editor, Laura Boss, who has trusted me with these papers, and to the wonderful people at The University of Akron Press, including Tom Bacher, Mary Biddinger, and Amy Freels, for believing in this project and for taking it on.

Currently, the papers Boss sent are residing in an old, off-white with gray trim suitcase with slightly rusting clasps that someone down the block from me put out by the curb one morning. I like the fact that these poems, rescued from the trash, are now in this suitcase, also rescued from the trash. It's been a great experience for me putting this book together. I hope you like it as much as I do.

References

Benedikt, Michael. Interview with Naomi Shihab. *Benedikt: A Profile*. Tucson: Grilled Flowers Press, 1977. Print.

Carroll, Paul, ed. *The Young American Poets*. Chicago: Follet Publishing, 1968. Print.

OF MICHAEL

Laura Boss

I met Michael Benedikt at the New York Book Fair in 1984. He was wearing a yellow and blue striped rugby shirt that I discovered over time he would almost always wear. He stopped at my table where I had copies of my poetry magazine, *Lips,* and began to talk to me in a way that was serious and flirtatious at the same time. The next day my phone rang and it was Michael. He asked if I'd drive into Manhattan to his Upper West Side apartment. I said yes and drove in to see him and would drive him around for the next twenty-three years, even though he told me David Ignatow had taught him to drive and that he had a driver's license. Michael said he was nervous about driving. After that first weekend, I often spent four days a week at Michael's apartment. At night, once I was asleep, Michael would write. He chain smoked and usually had a drink next to him and would usually sing along to Bob Dylan records while writing. He had a smoky voice, not so different from Bob Dylan's. Several years later, he also sang along to Bruce Springsteen cassettes. And often, around 4 a.m., he'd wake me and we'd dance together.

Michael often sat with a stub of a number 2 yellow pencil and revised poems—some that had already been published. He often worked at his computer on several manuscripts at the same time.

About a week after I met him, Michael said he wanted to visit his mother on Long Island who was up for the summer and staying at the brick beach bungalow where Michael had spent his childhood and teen summers. Michael was an only child, and his mother came up each summer from Florida to see him. When we got to Point Lookout, Michael told me he usually saw his mother once a year. Michael, though he loved his mother, also had a bit of a streak of rebellion when it came to her and bristled at her breakfast schedule. I remember his mother saying to him, "If you lose this girl, I'll never speak to you again." In retrospect, I realize her remark could have been the catalyst to his breaking up with me, but that he must have cared for me a lot more than his desire to rebel against his mother's directives.

Michael had that rare trait of being able to be emotionally intimate as well as physically intimate. Life with him was never boring on any level, and although I know it's often said about interesting people, Michael had a fresh, original way of perceiving things. He was one of those individuals who was more interesting talking about the weather than someone else who might be talking about the big bang theory, although Michael could talk about that too. In fact, when he was in middle school, he wrote a science paper that had so impressed his teachers that they sent him to various other New York City schools to deliver it.

Michael had gotten into the prestigious Stuyvesant High School, but chose not to go, he told me, because he felt it was too long a trip from his Bronx apartment in the High Bridge section where he lived with his parents. It was a long trip by subway, but most students would have grabbed the chance to go to Stuyvesant no matter how long the subway trip. One story from his youth that resonated with me was about him playing baseball. When he was young, he would watch his team's baseball game from his open apartment window. When it was his turn to bat, he would go outside, take his turn, and then go back in.

Michael didn't want to travel much. He would, in the early years, shop in the neighborhood. His big trips were to his dentist downtown and sometimes to poetry readings if either he or I was reading. Sometimes, though rarely, we'd go to museums like the Museum of Modern Art, and several times Michael took me to a birthday dinner at Mamasita's above the museum, which had a glamorous view of the city lights and minimalist decor. Michael knew it was my favorite city restaurant. But mostly we went to Hunan Balcony a block away from his apartment. And even more often, Michael had the food delivered. Michael would run around his apartment with a Dust Buster, vacuuming often, and Windexing his computer screen and French windows. Yet he was a major pack rat, with empty prescription bottles and boxes that VCRs or electric fans (etc.) had come in. He watched TV on a tiny screen on the table in his bedroom and watched a lot of PBS, but also watched *ER* and *Friends* sometimes. Michael and I only went to one movie in all our years together. It was a film about Bob Dylan and playing a block away.

Michael enjoyed music—from classical to rock. He often had WQXR on the radio. He had fond memories, he told me, of collaborating with his friend Michael Small, who wrote music for movies. Michael received an invitation to a reception at Lincoln Center for the director of a film that included one of the songs on which he and Michael Small had collaborated. I really wanted to go, but Michael didn't want to. Michael went out less and less it seemed each year, and when he chose to go out he was very selective. We did end up going to some wonderful parties, museums, and poetry readings.

Michael, before I knew him, had been poetry editor of the *Paris Review*, so we went to several parties at George Plimpton's townhouse (He later had a chance to return to editing, but he turned down the editorship of *Poetry* because he didn't want to move to Chicago.) I remember the way Plimpton had so many people over (many, like me, guests of those invited), and yet he left all these fascinating and valuable collectors items out—I loved the concept that assumed everyone would be trustworthy. Another *Paris Review* party to which Michael took me was one that Jackie Kennedy attended. Other parties to which Michael would always go were my mother's Thanksgiving bash at Mayfair Farms in New Jersey and some of my friends' holiday festivities. On our first Christmas Eve, we went to his friend Betty Kray's apartment and had dinner with Betty, her husband, Vladimir, and another friend of Betty's. Betty, who later would go on to found Poets House along with Stanley Kunitz, had been responsible for Michael hosting the 92nd Street Y Poetry Readings years before. Michael was fond of and admired Betty and felt very sad when she developed cancer, but visiting her was too difficult for him. One interesting aspect of Michael is that once he was outside his apartment and we were at a party or reading, he was sociable and charming, and usually one of the last to want to leave.

Until Michael got sick, we often spent weeks in the summer at Point Lookout once his mother died. And Michael would spend hours in the garden planting impatiens and marigolds and generally taking care of things. Sometimes, if I had workshops or family issues in New Jersey, I would go to my apartment there and then return to drive Michael back to the city or stay with him near the ocean. Michael was an intense gardener and gave that garden the same focus and concentration he gave his poems. Michael also spent time one year at Maspeth (his father's childhood home, left to Michael by his unmarried father's sister who had lived there) and got into a painting and repair project that eventually caused him serious problems with his West 98th Street landlord. Apparently, there was a tenant's law that said you could not spend more than a certain amount of time not living in your Manhattan apartment. In my opinion, the grief and hundreds of letters Michael spent writing to protest this, including court visits we did when possible, took a tremendous toll on Michael and his physical and mental energy. Michael even put up a website about his apartment problems.

And although there are many things Michael did not want to do, there were things Michael did chose to do. One thing for which Michael did not hesitate to travel was a reading at the Library of Congress. Gwendolyn Brooks, who didn't know him but knew his work, and as the equivalent of Poet Laureate, invited Michael to read. The huge honorarium was a definite incentive. Michael and I flew to Washington, D.C., and Brooks could not have been more welcoming.

Once his mother died, he had no further contact with his first cousins (who were his closest relatives) for sixteen years. Michael, in his last few years, virtually cut himself off from everyone. He rarely went down for his mail, and the letter carrier stopped delivering mail when there was no room left in the mailbox. Michael rarely answered the phone. I had always kept my New Jersey apartment on the Palisades above the Hudson River with its view of the New York skyline where I could see the outline of Michael's apartment more often than I was seeing him, although I still accompanied him to doctor's appointments, and he had my name listed as his emergency contact with his doctors. Michael was getting more and more reclusive, eventually even cutting off a visiting social worker who came for a while.

Even so, Michael continued to stay active on the Internet and on e-mail, and continued to work on his poems and website until just a few days before his death. At that time, Michael had a strong presence on the Internet. Michael was quick to figure out how to build a web page, and was proud of his technological skills and that Bob Holman had called him "The Poet Laureate of the Internet."

Michael often spoke about those poets he cared about but had cut himself off from, such as Robert Bly, James Tate, Charles Simic, Louis Simpson, Richard Howard, Eric Jong (whose poem to him he had framed on the kitchen wall), and William Matthews.

On the last day of his life, Michael was feeling really weak. He was using oxygen with an 'emergency' unlit cigarette nearby that I knew he would not touch. I brought in the medicine that had been delivered by the pharmacy.

I begged him to take the pills, but, horrible as he was feeling and as desperately as he needed the medicine, Michael stared at the bottle for several minutes, carefully reading everything on the label, even reading the possible side effects. After what seemed like an interminable amount of time, Michael opened the bottle and removed one pill and slowly put it in his mouth—taking it with a sip of the water I held out for him. His deliberate focus, even when so sick, was reminiscent of the way he was about everything. He didn't rush, no matter the circumstances. Even at the end, he wanted me to be certain to take the garbage out to the hall so the superintendent would pick it up. The practical side of Michael was a strong component of everything he did—whether it was writing, editing, or gardening, painting a wall or working on his taxes for six months.

The one major thing I did for Michael after he died was to save his papers and archives that were slated for the dumpster. Finally, the lawyer sent me thirteen boxes of Michael's archives: poems, photos, manuscripts, and more, which I now own.

And as I'm trying to capture this complex man I loved for decades, I can almost see Michael's ghost hovering close, taking out his sharpened stub of a yellow pencil and saying, "Laura, you need to go over this again," and he's probably right, as usual.

SIX PASSAGES

INTRODUCING MICHAEL BENEDIKT

Robert Archambeau

In the introduction to his 1976 book *The Prose Poem: An International Anthology*, Michael Benedikt defines the prose poem as having six special qualities: an attentiveness to the unconscious; a impression of external reality as something mediated by our inner worlds; a feeling for the fluctuations of consciousness; a commitment to colloquial speech; a sense of humor; and a "hopeful skepticism" (49). Benedikt's selections in the anthology give this definition a surprising degree of credence, but Benedikt's list doesn't just describe the style of the prose poem: it provides the best possible brief definition of the qualities of his own writing, in poetry and prose poetry alike.

1

> *The image is a pure creation of the mind. It cannot be born from a comparison but from a juxtaposition of two more or less distant realities. The more the relationship between the two juxtaposed realities is both distant and true, the stronger the image will be. . . .*
>
> *—Pierre Reverdy, "The Image"*

Benedikt came by his interest in the unconscious through a long, deep, and fruitful engagement with Surrealism. Encouraged by Robert Bly in 1963 to investigate Surrealism, Benedikt became devoted to French Surrealism in particular, and in the early sixties alternated between undertaking translations from the French and writing his own poems, as if deliberately seeking the guidance of the Surrealist tradition. Indeed, by the time Benedikt's anthology *The Poetry of Surrealism* appeared in 1974, he had become one of the leading American experts on Surrealist writing. So central had Surrealism become to his sense of what was most valuable in literature that, in his introduction to the anthology, he recruited his immediate influences (New York School poets like Frank O'Hara, John Ashbery, and Kenneth Koch) and his favorite poets from the English Romantic school (Wordsworth and Coleridge) to the Surrealist camp. Benedikt eventually became wary of being too closely identified with Surrealism, though, claiming in 1977 that Surrealism was no longer central to his work. But, as the poems in the present volume attest, from the earliest to the latest work, his poetry frequently alternates or fuses passages of dream reality with empirical reality, following the proto-Surrealist Pierre Reverdy's description of the process by which strong images are born via the juxtaposition of distant realities.

2

> *Modernity in the broadest sense, as it has asserted itself historically, is reflected in the irreconcilable opposition between sets of values corresponding to (1) the objectified, socially measurable time of capitalist civilization... and (2) the personal, subjective, imaginative durée, the private time created by the unfolding of the "self."*
>
> —*Matei Calinescu,* Five Faces of Modernity

A confirmed agoraphobe, Benedikt was always more than ordinarily attuned to the boundaries between the public world of objective events and the world of private experience. In an interview with Naomi Shihab, Benedikt spoke of how the problem of communication for the poet had to do with "bringing the internal world and the external world together," linking or "playing off or perhaps testing the language of travel folders, the language of banking, of instruction manuals" against another world altogether, the world of "internal, 'personal,' or psychological things" (9). This, he goes on to say, is "not only an aesthetic imperative but a moral imperative" (11). We get a sense, from this comment, of just how seriously Benedikt took the fusing of dream and external realities. There are moments in his work, though, when the moral imperative to connect the inner and the outer seems almost too great for him to bear.

Consider *Mole Notes,* the most sustained and most powerfully imagined work in Benedikt's oeuvre. This sequence of prose poems represents something approaching a total retreat from the external world. Here, the world out there is dangerous, and the tunneling Mole retreats in pessimism to a world of the literal and psychological underground. One understands the urge to retreat, especially given the events of 1971, the year in which *Mole Notes* appeared: the Weather Underground bombing of the Capitol building; the conviction of both Charles Manson and of the American lieutenant found guilty in the Mai Lai massacre; the arrest of 12,000 antiwar protestors; the Pentagon Papers bringing to light corruption and cynicism at the highest levels; genocide in Bangladesh; the prison riots at Attica; and the continuing specter of nuclear annihilation looming over the entire planet. If, as Benedikt claimed in his interview with Shihab, *Mole Notes* and his next book, *Night Cries*, represented a "black pessimism" (26), it was pessimism well grounded in events.

It was also a pessimism that faded, and the poems of *The Badminton at Great Barrington; or Gustave Mahler & the Chattanooga Choo-Choo* find Benedikt once again fearlessly exploring the boundary between the subjective and the objective realms, this time giving us a protagonist who, unlike Mole, is excessively drawn to the excitements and allures of the external world.

3

> *Their purpose of writing was to portray, not a thought, but a mind thinking, or, in Pascal's words, la peinture de la pensée. They knew that an idea separated from the act of experiencing is not the idea that was experienced. The ardor of its conception in the mind is a necessary part of its truth....*
>
> —*Morris W. Croll, "The Baroque Style in Prose"*

In an essay much-loved and quoted by poets as diverse as Elizabeth Bishop and Charles Bernstein, the critic Morris W. Croll described the tenor and technique of baroque prose, which eschewed classical reserve for "the energy and labor of minds seeking the truth, not without dust and heat" (208). Benedikt's work frequently proceeds in the baroque manner, showing the probings of the conscious mind as well as the interweaving of the rational and the irrational. Not for Benedikt the paring down of an initial prolixity into the austere perfection of the *mot juste* in the manner of, say, the young Ezra Pound when, over the course of a year, he cut the thirty-six lines of an initial draft down to the spare couplet that is "In a Station of the Metro." Instead, Benedikt shows the mind working to find the right expression. Consider "INVITATION TO PREVIOUSLY UNINVITED GUESTS" from *Mole Notes*, in which the smoke of a rare cigar melting into a room full of guests is described as being "like a sugar cube melting on the tongue" and "like honey in the mind of a diabetic" (101), similes that launch a long catalog of other comparisons:

> ...like your wallet in the hands of a prostitute, like chopped liver in the heart of the professional caterer, like surviving leaves in midwinter sleet, like ant feces in a vat full of nitrate, like an inexpensive tieclip before the onslaughts of rust, like conversation into silence among boring company, like the conception of generosity after December 26th, like space beneath even the tiniest hand caressing even the tallest lover discovering the joys of some novel perversion, like the idea of 18th-century chamber music in the minds of the oppressed, like truth in a Latin-American newspaper, like dialogue in the mouth of the megalomaniac, like meaning in the mind of the poet. (101)

What we see here is the mind of the poet seeking the *mot juste*, rather than the *mot juste* itself. While there's a certain humorous quality to the proliferation of similes—when we arrive at the final image of meaning dispersing like smoke in the mind of the poet, we've reached a point of comic exasperation—there's a serious purpose to Benedikt's method. Just as he saw exploring the intersection of the inner and outer worlds as a moral imperative, he saw depicting the mind in thought as a moral as well as an aesthetic matter. His representation of the mind's processes, he claimed in the Shihab interview, had to do with "incorporating more and more and the incorporation doesn't make you *lose* focus... but rather makes you get a greater part of your mind *in* focus" (20). For Benedikt, if one is to write truthfully, one must write the process of the mind into the poem.

4

> *That's part of Personism. It was founded by me after lunch with LeRoi Jones on August 27, 1959, a day in which I was in love with someone (not Roi, by the way, a blond). I went back to work and wrote a poem for this person. While I was writing it I was realizing that if I wanted to I could use the telephone instead of writing the poem, and so Personism was born. It's a very exciting movement which will undoubtedly have lots of adherents. It puts the poem squarely between the poet and the person, Lucky Pierre style, and the poem is correspondingly gratified. The poem is at last between two persons instead of two pages. In all modesty, I confess that it may be the death of literature as we know it.*
>
> *—Frank O'Hara, "Personism: A Manifesto"*

The comic quality of Benedikt's work comes with an impressive pedigree. An exclamation-mark laden, buoyant, faux-naïve quality is especially evident in the earlier work, which was very much written in the shadow of Frank O'Hara and Kenneth Koch, whose works the young Benedikt would often read for an hour or so before setting down to write his own poems. A decade or so younger than the leading poets of the New York School, Benedikt was, like most of the more established poets, a Francophile, an Ivy Leaguer, and a professional art critic. Like them, too, he tended to write with an awareness of the hip, knowing intimacy of the New York poetry scene. He's not above dropping a proper name or two in a poem, and once you start counting the pronouns in Benedikt's poetry, you'll be surprised at how many times you'll find "you," "we," and "us;" both of these are techniques that help to build a sense of reader-writer community. Indeed, much of the charm and warmth of Benedikt's comic gestures depend on one's sense of being taken into a little imaginative circle, where we communicate as intimates. His is a poetry that cracks a wry smile in a small room, rather than sounding a barbaric yawp over the rooftops of the world.

5

> *The principal object, then, proposed in these Poems was to choose incidents and situations from common life, and to relate or describe them, throughout, as far as was possible in a selection of language really used by men, and, at the same time, to throw over them a certain coloring of imagination....*
>
> —*William Wordsworth, "Preface to* Lyrical Ballads*"*

Benedikt was prone to abuse T. S. Eliot in his critical writings, and one understands why. Unlike Eliot, whose strongest work could read like a polyglot tissue of quotations from classic or arcane texts, Benedikt insisted on a certain plainspokenness, an ordinary language as the medium for poetry. He complained in *Poetry* about poets who asserted their bardic privilege, which was really nothing more than a "bardic abuse," whose method was tediously "'kultural,' involving ponderously 'literary' phrases or phrases whose grace is meant to astonish, representing, by stuffing implication, the poetic soul" (109). This is not to say that Benedikt limits his range of diction to that of the ordinary man on the street, as the high incidence of the romantic exclamatory or classically apostrophic "oh!" in his writing makes plain. What Benedikt does, though, is to shy away from the notion of the poet as a kind of collagist piecing together the fragments of tradition, and insist on language that appears to be the expression of a speaking subject, a talker talking to us. The notion is at least as venerable as Wordsworth and as modern as Frank O'Hara, with his idea that the telephone can replace the poem—and it is an idea Benedikt inherits from both poets.

6

A particularly perceptive analysis of Benedikt's *Mole Notes* contains the following passage:

> *Ironically, what Mole seeks by way of unreason is a more reasonable, rationally utopian world. Throughout the poem... Mole's dominant emotion is, as Benedikt puts it, disappointment.... Mole-Benedikt cannot locate or establish Mole City on earth as it is; he finds only war, riots, crime, delusion. The great climax of the poem occurs therefore in what the poet calls Mole's apotheosis, his literal flying through space like a projectile. What in the individual man amounts to a personal Thoreauvian-like revolt must perforce divorce him from society.*
>
> —*Louis Gallo, "Benedikt's Blues: Reason and Unreason in Poetry"*

The passage captures the hopeful skepticism of Benedikt's work: skeptical of any great claims for poetry or the renewal of the world, his poetry remains optimistic about the power and prospects of the individual imagination. Even after he had given up on many things—academe, fame, even the publication of his work—Benedikt could ask in "RITA & RINGO" that we

> ... suppose then that, following our sudden realizations & quasi-
> epiphanies, madly inspired
> With our eyes rolling around wildly, our tongue hanging out & our
> hair standing up on end despite the breeze,
> One of us rushes to our clattery, old-fashioned,
> pre-computer-era typewriter,
> To make at least a temporary little household racket...

Even if this racket might "Risk being mistaken by some for a 'Throwaway Poem'" that the poet writes only "for the light amusement of himself or herself & perhaps a few old friends," ("RITA & RINGO") it remains the medium of enthusiasm and hair-raising enthusiasm. And even if the unpublished poems were tucked away in a suitcase, the hope remained—it is there in that line about the poem being "mistaken" as something only for the poet's friends—that they would find their way out into the world, to you.

References

Benedikt, Michael. "The Apotheosis of Darkness *Vs.* Bardic Privilege." *Poetry* Nov. 1972: 109. Print.

———. Interview with Naomi Shihab. *Benedikt: A Profile*. Tucson: Grilled Flowers Press, 1977. Print.

———. *Mole Notes*. Middletown: Wesleyan University Press, 1971. Print.

———. "RITA & RINGO." http://www.angelfire.com/ny/MichaelBenedikt/rngorit2.html. Web.

Benedikt, Michael, ed. *The Prose Poem: An International Anthology*. New York: Dell, 1976. Print.

Croll, Morris W. "The Baroque Style in Prose." *Style, Rhetoric, and Rhythm: Essays by Morris W. Croll*. Ed. J. Max Patrick. Princeton: Princeton University Press, 1961. 208. Print.

PREFACE TO *BENEDIKT: A PROFILE* (1977)

Michael Benedikt

Poetry for me is, finally, irreducibly, a way of knowing. It is not so much "knowledge," in the final, conventional sense—valuable as that surely is—but knowledge in process; or, rather, self-knowledge in process. Sometimes, in writing poetry, it seems that the further along that road one travels, the longer the road stretches out, and the littler one's feeling of whatever one may have learned. But I find that to be a sense that keeps life interesting. "Keeps"? The word is too static, too functional. That sense of process is probably, for me, nothing less than the raw materials of life.

Whether the art that comes out of this feeling should be interesting to anybody else is another question; or is it? Obviously, the internal integrity of the work of art in itself (whether individual poem or individual book or individual whatever) is what one hopes, first and finally, will appeal to other people. Yet on another level, I think I'm hoping that the reader will take pleasure in the process of self-understanding, which one wants to relate to others besides the person who is trying to do the aforementioned understanding. I suppose I believe that there is a kind of community of pleasure, as well as pain.

I understand that my poems have changed over the years, moving from relatively objective constructions toward something else. Increasingly, they are a matter of searchings, gropings, and of downright pratfalls, at least on the psychological level. I believe that there is a closer relationship between the confession/revelation of personal character and even error, and the possibility of the esthetically authentic, than I ever dared think before. Increasingly, too, I feel that the "techniques" I write in (which are probably becoming more various not less, precisely as I focus in on the kind of work I want to do) are *necessities* for me. They choose me, at least as much as I have consciously chosen them.

Perhaps this already says more about what I think I'm doing than I already know; after all, this little preface is being written after the poems were written. Still, I think the poems point towards these feelings; and if they do not, I am painfully aware that there are always the jokes to fall back on.

OF POETRY, MY FRIEND

OK, poems, I haven't written any of you lately, for what seems like almost at least an eon
To me, although for all I know nobody out there may be exactly throwing, in fits & starts, a random tantrum
About your absence. Indeed, for all I know, there may even be no
Publisher, like a perpetual vacuum-cleaner,
Dying, just, for my latest stardust. Still, I need you, poetry—your sometimes outrageous explorations, your often preposterous revelations, to tell me, poetry, precisely
Just what I'm doing. "Just What I'm Doing"
Sometimes remains hidden from me as if in a silken
Blindfold, like a secret guest panelist
On some TV guessing-game; or else concealed worse than some flirt behind her fan, unless a little art, finally
Tells me who what & where I am. Am I myself, perhaps
"The Scarlet Pimpernel," who's got himself into the world's worst pickle
With his endless, masked disguises? Have I really
Lived through anything recently, & have I, after all, after all this time

Really learned anything? Have I been listening to even the least little thing? &, in the very midst of things, has there been anything happening
Worth mentioning? Oh, it can pour out such a crazy cornucopia
Of accusation, or (sometimes) occasional confirmation— "It" (I mean you, poetry)
Which can tell without fail the vast & all-important difference 'twixt a merely hollow silo & a truly perforated void
At the first breath of any reborn metaphor, potent consonant, or vital verb
& Thus uncover a person in all their "Guiltiness" or maybe somewhat groggy "Glory"
Or else announce some other, maybe smaller, but nonetheless still resounding truth, should neither of those two terms apply.

Well, we've all known those days which seem so externally uneventful
That somehow just noodling around on the psychological saxophone
Is enough—which is why, personally, I like you, poetry: you're friendly;
You hang around with even spiritual drifters, on even the meanest of
streetcorners
& Act sometimes like the kind of just-for-kicks pickpocket
Who will klepto your watchfob, then return it;
& Slap you on the back thereafter; & buy you a beer.

So, for your curious gentleness, too, poetry, I guess there's a lot to be said for
you (or at least there certainly should be)
Even though in those thoughts & words you may sometimes bless the best,
There may be all the discretion, & some of the forbearance, of the
professional strangler.
Monolithic, stoney sorrow, or merely floppy joy; & in general, a pure if
possibly unpopular admixture
Of things yet-to-be-revealed, or maybe better yet, left unsaid.

Poetry, you don't just come right out & say: "Look, baby, today I looked over
& across all of reality
& Also athwart your heart, where the whole of this great big world including
a whole lotta things lots more obvious than you
Had been pressed up quite hard against it
& Found that a great big hole was starting to form in it!"

—Which is nice of you, poetry, who I hope will remain my friend.

from

Changes: A Chapbook

RAISING

Raising our grapes on the side
Of this vast hill
We realize what it is to ski.
We press our grapes lovingly
As we think of the passages,
The swirls of weather, the slicing
Upon the big barren ground.
There is no sun, no charming
Girls in picking costumes.
Suddenly I realize too
The similarity to ice skating.

LANDSCAPE

At my whistle, with your basket
Superior to all the village others
You come bounding down
Jingling like little monies
From all over the world.
When you fall asleep, it is like growing.
Patronage is no use. I love your empty baskets
Woven with funeral wreaths
And I will never leave this village.
I will not know the world
Except as a magazine.

THE GIFT STEEDS

Here come the steeds I said I'd send
Now! There they are rolling them by
In barrels, the air is full of the looks
Of the steeds, sardonic, bemused.
And you are pleased! Here is a lemon
To keep. And here is a ribbon
For a bookmark, unless you will use
A steed. For how otherwise
Are you likely to use them? To hold down a corner
Of a magazine, to keep the page, to examine
Passages before you use them, in
The water? Every one should do a whinny
And you would realize what power
Is, realize, dear, that these steeds
Are the little symbols of my liking.

VICTORIA FALLS

Our window is covered by the beard
Of the man overhead
Leaning out the window
Watching the jewel-thieves;
The door is useless as a hatch.
The house is moving slowly
Toward Victoria Falls
Place of melancholy and humor and destruction.
Will you comfort me with the soddenness
Of your cheeks at night,
Of your eyes,
Of your harmless webbed feet.

IRONIES

Here is some hat wax. Remember
To keep it by your elbow, knock
It onto your shoulder, Paul.
Here is a raven's beak: recall
To get caught in it and, bleeding,
Run surprised to the doctor some night.
There is a ship, its smoke
Upon your pillow like a fog.
How will you avoid being lost?

SURVIVOR

Here are some rocks that are falling
On you. It is the history of the world
You are reading, hand on the dog.
They are falling around your shelves,
About the fireplace. They will hit China,
Linen, the portrait of the perished
Aunt perched on the mantelpiece.
Afterwards, cleaning them away
You will sweep the dog under the carpet
With that expression of deep shock.

CONSOLATION

Are you feeling paltry this morning
Jogging up and down the roadway
Without a head? The morning mists
Sweep across your shoulders like capes
As you approach me making motions
What can I say to you, except: don't look at me
That way, or, we are all very sorry,
Or, why don't you sit down on some stone,
Catch your breath? I am sorry
You feel weary, but remember, I am
Sitting here a bit uncomfortably:
We all must share in implacable fate.

CHANGES

Why is this grass so hideous
This year, as compared, say
To the clouds in the sky,
Which retain their moisture.
I understand these trees keep
Lovelier birds every year.
This grass I can only laugh at.
Some day I feel it will lengthen
Lushen and densify
And we will sit on it with calm hearts
Under the clouds, which will be rotten,
And have a little picnic.

from

The Body

AIR

Air, air, you are the distantmost thing I know,
Not even the whales in their patterns upon and under
The sea, are more inscrutable, to me;
You carry sails of travelers to interesting places,
And adventurers, sailors, or just plain traders;
You encourage the bicyclist to mount his apparatus
And you are ever present during swimming lessons
So that when the reluctant swimmer may emerge
From the water an instant, he'll freeze;
And air, you are hanging around fetid places
Always, ready to clear the dank atmosphere
With a breath of yourself; I have found you in
The slums of the intellect even, about to puff
When the mind is hopelessly weak after travel,
And in the lines of poems, pointless to all others,
Poised like a bouquet, sprightly and colorful.

London, 1962

THE EUROPEAN SHOE

The European Shoe is constructed of grass and reed, bound up and wound around so that it may slip easily over the wearer's head.

In case you are an aircraft pilot, you must take care that the European Shoe does not creep off your foot, and begin to make its way carefully along the fuselage.

The European Shoe pressed against the fugitive's nose, preventing it from imminent departure.

The European Shoe spends summers in delightful ways. A lady feels its subtle and unexpected pressure the length of her decolletage. (It winters in pain.)

That time I lent you my European Shoe you departed with a look of grandeur, and in total disrepair.

The European Shoe knocks on the door of the carefree farmerette. "The harvest has been gathered in, ha, ha," it says, moving shyly forth along the edge of the couch.

I pointed to the European Shoe. I ate the European Shoe. I married the European Shoe.

Tears fall from the eye of the European Shoe as it waves goodbye to us from the back balcony of the speeding train.

It helps an old lady, extremely crippled and arthritic, move an enormous cornerstone. It invents a watch, which, when wound up tightly, flies completely to pieces.

It was a simple and dignified ceremony, distinguished for its gales of uncontrollable laughter, in which I married the European Shoe.

If it rains, the European Shoe becomes very heavy. I failed to cross the river, where thousands of European Shoes lay capsized.

And so we lived alone, we two, the envy of our neighborhoods, the delight of our lively hordes of children.

I saw a flightful of graceful swallows heading to distant, half-forgotten islands over the distant seas; and in the midst of that annually questing company, I saw the European Shoe.

It never harmed anyone, and yet it never helped anyone.

Gaily it sets out into the depths of my profoundest closet, to do battle with the dusts of summer.

FRAUDULENT DAYS

Fraudulent days, the surfaces collapse
When against them you press your finger
The beautiful brick suit
When you scrape it is only a tinsel clothing
The whole upper stories of the building
Touched, is a seagull's back, revealed

And when I press in on you with my shynesses,
An acceleratedly decreasing circle,
Your eyes look up as if to discourage
Departure. Your eyelids constantly falling
Under the lampshade, beneath this greenish light
In this wholly improvised conviction

PROCESSION

Now that I notice it is my much beloved body which has been drifting back
and forth beneath the pier underwater
I am becoming more sympathetic to snails
After all, what do oysters want
Seals are shy
And what is the matter with putting up a playful fin among the swimmers

Thus we march forward into a future
Arms akimbo legs akimbo head akimbo
Hair akimbo as it gradually drifts away
There is so much that is akimbo here that there is hardly any room to be
"awry"

Forward forward forward
Into a privileged area where a curious conglomeration
Of currents and sand has made out a little space
Out of the wind out of the rain out of the unmanageable crowds
Who flow over the sense of privacy, and among whom
Any umbrella is easily lost

Some day all things will be water that battleship
Which you see bounding on the main will be liquid or gaseous
Its captain and its crew
The spinster with her what-not shelves the teamster with his graft
The subways with their calming quality the grass with its disturbances
Lapels with all their pallor and graveyards with their sheen

All will be water all will be pouring
Descending from the skein of the firm and the packed
There is no pleasanter exercise on earth than metamorphosis
Time passes
And all the things that we love must be changed

THE EYE

The narcissist's eye is blue, fringed with white and covered with tempting salad leaves.

The purse-stealer's eye is yellow.

The eye of the non-combatant is white. In the center is a target rendered in green and black.

The voluptuary's eye comes to a point. It is like a silo, the echo of a halo.

The gravedigger's eye is hollow. It is surrounded by a thoroughly contemporary serenity.

The dynamite salesman's eye is like a pool, in which he who leans to drink may be lost. Drifting forever, like a cloud.

The maiden's eye is tucked under.

The billiard-player's eye comes to a point. It is like a mild wine. Each billiard-player suffers from imperfect nostalgia.

The ghost's eye is green.

The poet's eye is like a candy.

The battleship captain's eye is like the light that falls in a glen, when the doe has done with drinking.

The eye of the realist is inflatable.

HIDING-PLACE

It is a haven climbing here under
Your hand, as it moves across the porch
Thumbing among the magazines, selecting,
As it dips into the pit of the night
And grasps the wrist of the departing.
I wish I could be one of your lovers
And could bring you food and rings
Good news and stationery,
Photographs and improved climate.
I would climb out from under your fingertips
And would leap from knee to knee.
You would surely supply me with dust particles then
For me to drop on all these beetles;
And I would roll them down mountainsides
And listen for the crushing noise.
Together we would forge a mode of life.
They would find us hidden under the sea
Just after the earth entirely collapsed,
A situation I hope will never obtain.
I like it here very much now.

DEVELOPMENTS

1.
Suddenly we were overwhelmed with genuine reasons
Several of us were impressed
And one of our company threw open the window

"It was nice! It was nice!"

We had never liked it more than that previously.

2.
That night, gathered around the candlesticks
We examined it.
It raised its little head and smiled back in return

And we made it our official mascot.

3.
Now we gradually tire of our ancient playthings.
They keep coming to our attention,
Other items. Our meetings differ

How can we help investigating them?

I myself begin to feel that we must retire from our previous enthusiasms.

4.
This morning, the largest newspaper in the universe
Carries a headline saying

It has died during the night
Of love.

GEMINI EMBLEM

I was so undecided
I seemed constantly to be leaping to my feet and then sitting down in one
incredibly powerful motion

People stopped in front of my location
To observe the phenomena

Besides that, I couldn't sleep,
Bit my nails, felt dizzy after dancing,
And I had this picture in my mind of carrying around my lungs as if they
were valises I was trying to smuggle through customs, perhaps as if to
slip my heart through my mind

There I was, at thirty,
A blur on the horizon.

A BELOVED HEAD

A beloved head, truly, but the mouth part was operated
By a small treadle
Located just outside near the corner of the lawn;
The ears by a lightswitch
And the eyes by two faucets, mounted inside the writingdesk.
The hair was operated by a kind of abacus
On which one tried not to lose count of possible developments there;
When it hung down loose it could envelop the attention of the operator.

The body of the beloved was operated from an enormous panel
Covered with hundreds of dials
One had to climb up to it by means of a ladder
Daring that only after a refresher-course from the handbook which came
with either the previous instrument, or the previous beloved, the
operator can never remember which
How often that body would suddenly whirl around
With a gesture so gentle and rare
One could not seriously comprehend that one had created it

—Nor even the way it arched its back and stretched
in the commonest of yawns; or adjusted jewelry
come slightly awry (one had accidentally brushed
against a small throttle located near the knee)—

And sometimes the controlling mind collapses.
Just look at the way the operator is slumped over now.
He is tired, his head hurts, his hand is exhausted
In fact he has fallen asleep there in his chair.
And the beloved, head and body, is passing the time until the next
awakening
By sitting around and sewing, presently the sleeve
Of a doll's kimono which she has decided to give to a Japanese friend of hers
who collects such things

SOME FEELINGS

The feelings go up into the air
Rising in lines that are straight until they bump
Into something
A building
With its roof overhanging, a judge
Who is looking out of the window attempting to see that nurse
Changing uniforms which are transparent anyway in a neighboring indoor
    hospital yard
Music (the feelings sift through little drifting notes from a radio);
Then they continue
Rising so swiftly and so purely they seem to supersede all objects

Only somebody
At the level of the ground may see
That each feeling is connected by a thread to a forehead, an arm, or a leg
And that individuals
At the heights of their tragic moments
Resemble porcupines or pincushions.

JOY

How can I get through that innocence?
Jump through, and land in a damp swamp?
No, I'd rather go bicycling

Around, and enjoy its transparent squalor
Starred with flowers so magnificent
Only the most rotted self-deception could impel them.

Another thing I like doing a lot
Is helping you across busy boulevards
With a specially enlargeable hand

Implying friendly aid at first,
Secondly, a growing degree of passion;
Then I inflate it and make it throb! I also enjoy

Watching you tremble in deserted underground tunnels,
Your wonderful trembling too when we are side by side at midnight,
And kayaking in mid-Atlantic, alone.

AT NIGHT

The things left undone
Are looking at us with their enquiring glances

They see through our schedule
They know we have been putting them off a lot

That somewhere
The things done
Are sitting around, listening to my record-player, smoking my cigars,
    wearing my slippers, and drinking wine from my long-stemmed
    glasses, and feeling very well in general
Because they are the things attended to initially.

It's arbitrary, though: I would just as soon have kissed you behind the thigh
    where your hair starts to become unexpectedly curly
As on that particular spot beneath your ear which curves like a rowboat
Overturned and found
On a steep beach
At night.

THOUGHTS

Excuse me, isn't that you I see concealed underneath there
Inside the shield, or conning tower, of your head,
Your eyes looking out of the perforations in your flesh?
How can you think you can see from out of liquid, anyway? Are rain puddles
 watching me even now,
And can ducts which punctuate the underground of a field
Examine it at will for buried treasure? Is the rain outside your window a
 voyeur, then? Deep down under all that, though,
Underneath the liquids and the various unobservant stuffs,
There is a spirit, shifting around from foot to foot.

AFTER A READING OF MCLUHAN, WHOM I ADMIRED

Will you complain about old-fashioned furniture?
Forever, a mode of knowing
Will be retained on the inside of the human head,
But the furniture will gradually embarrass you
And tomorrow you may throw it away.

If only it were possible for a person to recline on a planet
Using the north polar ice cap as an ottoman,
The south polar cap as a pouf,
And the equator as a kitchen. It would crowd the house;
Yet the brain is never quite occupied.

The changes going on around outside the building here
Leave the brain the same blue lump it always was;
You may try to adjust but always truly contemporary events
Will be judged with thoughts a little older than they are;
Throw away your head

THE BATHROOM MIRROR

Nothing is going to get elucidated any more around here, we rely
On the natural course of events to explain itself;
And the way we are leaning forward, shading our ears and cupping our eyes
And the blank looks on our faces
Tell us not what we need to know, but only
Who it is that is looking and listening

The bathroom mirror is revealed as the site of revelation
At 11:35 p.m., on the last Friday of October, 1967, its truth is told
The truth of the bathroom mirror with its toothbrushholder, its
    fingermarked water glasses, the twisted toothpaste tube, the false
    eyelashes and the razor
Revelation revelation
Revelation of the thing we have always been closest to.
Now, without our having to ask it to, it shows us all the depth of the things
    we have known and loved the best

PYROMANIAC'S LAMENT IN SPRING

in memory, Dr. M. L. King

"I see, I see
In spite of all my hard work, *them*
Returned and resumed.
Like a flame coming across burning floorboards, stepped on repeatedly,
harder and harder, faster and faster
They are a danger;
As much a danger as if flowers began to flourish from roadside lumps of
debris

"Already I see a pair of busy hands taking up stitching and knitting needles,
thrown down into their wicker bowl as the curtains caught;
The ladder with blackened top step and broken rungs below is removed
from the second-story windowsill and placed back in the garage;
Pieces of broken glass, lying like jewels on the lawn, leap back up to form a
bathroom window;
Shoes left behind as the inhabitants tried to flee want to be refitted to feet;
The switched-off old stove that exploded anyway is turned on again, the
odors of the strange vegetables and fleshes of that black house begin
to permeate the street, back, black;
Slyly returned to the bedroom wall is the poster you could see from the
street of the nude, all belly, white and gleaming;
Blades of grass begin to prickle the ground near the basement window from
which, years ago, good horizontals of cleansing flame once emerged;
Fine hair is restored;
A Saint Bernard big enough to ride, trapped once behind a locked screen
door, walks the floor again. Its back and shoulders are tingling
And from the heaps of knitting still to be completed emerges a single baby's
bootie in bright red."

OLD SCHOOL TIES

It's difficult in this maze of footsteps of friends superannuated to keep
track.
It somewhat resembles the attempt to constantly calculate where every
mouse may be in a deserted cheese-works behind the city dump, so as
to be able to reply sharply at any given instant, in case an inspector
comes by with his cap and his clip-board at the ready
Or maybe it's more like juggling with trick clubs that fall apart with every
other throw. But I hear them constantly tiptoeing backward,
Inside the remains of the lives we occupied when we knew one another
better
But never coming out into the new life, which is interesting because it is
difficult not to become dead in sooner.

When will it be possible again to share the richness of how little we had
experienced?
How soon will the new life begin?

THE GUARDIAN ANGEL

The guardian angel spreads out his wings and they stretch from the
department store on the corner to the Riverside Park gazebo
His feet are in the middle of 98th Street at the center of the sidewalk in
front of my building
He has been there since I came here, examining me for extravagances,
inspecting, and dictating the proper phrases to use in Poetry
He arranged for my last writing assignment, the one that paid reasonably
well, the intellectual job, the one for the *Chinese Opera Flower Gazette.*
Someday, when I am one hundred, I know he will arrange suitable
employment as poet-in-residence atop the Empire State Building or
else establish my chair as Gardener at Bennington.
There he is, hunched up in silhouette against the streetlight.
As I pass by this cold morning at 6 a.m., twirling my top hat on my reveler's
cane, I try to shake his wing to say hello finally for the first time, and
ask him in out of the snow that is obviously going to fall

New York, 1967

from

Sky

THE FUTURE

The future is withdrawn again.
Just as the donkey's teeth are pressing against the carrot, somebody removes the donkey.
If this is all the future holds for our nation's donkeys we may never make it through the forthcoming year!
What we need is a future in which vegetable gardens are planted in the atmosphere.
Gnash gnash.
Each step of the way must be marked by a half-eaten tuber or legume tossed aside, as if luxury were everyday
Or, as if donkeys could now go in any direction they wanted, even into the past.

Advancing on all sides, listen to the delicate steppings and droppings of the donkeys, catching up to the future, making the past come alive sooner and sooner.
When the future is finally achieved, the valley of the world will see, strewn as far as the eye can see, donkeys sitting down or lying around at their ease, little carts unhitched and parked; we will be aware as never before of the portability of time

CLEMENT ATTLEE

1.

Except for me, almost nobody remembers Clement Attlee.

The winds of change and cold snows, too, have flowed all over his features and figure, and now all we can see is a Sherlock Holmes cap and large pair of earmuffs.

Occasionally, a bear comes by and finds a boot to bite.

Oh, wake up Clement Attlee, another inch of time and not only will no one admit to remembering you, but nobody will be able to be found who has ever heard of you!

Clement, Clement!—Hi ho, first post-war English Labourite and somewhat socialist Prime Minister—hi ho, hoo-hoo.

2.

The other day, in the moviehouse (after all these years, *I* should say "cinema"?) a hundred people chuckled when a French general with large weights affixed to his eyelids said he had once been a member of the "underground resistance."

Upstairs, twelve students from nursery school are discussing the New Order.

At a party, I finally meet God. He is with a student. He's embarrassed, he grimaces a lot (the student).

Elsewhere, a graduate of Sarah Lawrence College is entering a mosque.

Apocalypse!

3.

In bed—place from which all creation is sent forth—I feel a shiny bald head with a bristly walrus moustache upon my pillow

And under the coverlet, sense that suddenly I'm wearing checquered knickers and carrying a walking stick.

Cautiously, a frayed black monocle-cord starts to make its way back across my cheek...

MONEY

Funny money. It giggles as it goes. Whenever we are about to spend some,
just as we reach into our pockets, it goes "Ho Ho!"
Inklings may come to us that it is attempting to soothe us at the expense of
the truth, for after all, even to money that giggles there is an end.
But we go along with its masquerade, since we want to do what makes it
happiest.
Yes!—we want bills of large and small denominations both to flutter with
laughter in our hands
We want dimples on the face of all currencies, coins to be smiling as they are
slipped into slots
Every vending machine to be regarded as a cornucopia of jokes and mirth,
mankind receiving a smile with every gumball, candy bar, soft drink,
seat cover, pocket comb, cigarette, foot vibration, etc.
Gaiety residing in change purses and pockets,
Piggy banks should squeal to be broken.
When we walk into a bank, we want to hear tittering from the tellers' cages
Muffled chuckles from safe deposit vaults
High hilarity from the halls
And the whole littered with packets of newly mined bills and rolls of
pennies and silver throwing themselves around on the floor,
guffawing.

But see how the ungracious bank guards seem indifferent to our ambition.
Ever they face the doors, front and rear, regular or revolving, with guns at
the ready.
Ever the shopkeeper will throw his body without hilarity over the cash
register as we enter with our fame,
And vending-machine franchisers are taking special care to affix locks
tightly to their product, and its goods,
While stockbrokers chew on pencils eternally, with sad looks.

Tears every night create the river of our true hope and faith
Upon which borne along gravely is the contemporary barque of utter
financial solvency

THE BLOCKHOUSE

In the blockhouse at the far end of the field where the powerful new bomb
was being tested
The reverberations of the damage we do just arrived;

See how the brilliant young scientist standing next to the panel of dials
drops his cup of coffee
While the experienced old engineer is tilted, and falls within the broom
closet
The pretty young typist in the corner who is staring at the framed
photograph of her boyfriend feels her eyes disastrously deflected
directly onto the page in her typewriter
And observe how the Fuller Brush Man who has just entered the blockhouse
feels his goods in their attaché case ominously jiggle
Just as a trembling comes over the green spears of a plant that has been
thriving there upon the radiator

Even the janitor swallows his gum
Even the uniformed guard drops his gun
Even the charlady lets the fuzz escape from her dustcloth, that impeccable
and portable dump.
And oh! I just noticed a mouse who happened to be watching all this from
the mousehole doorsill with his five small mice and their mother
Run hysterically away, the seven pink mousetails vanishing.

A family; I don't even have a family

THE ARTILLERY PORTRAIT

Each cannon when it fired
Shot out a little cannon

Or else the smoke took the shape of the kind of gun
From which it came;

Or else the smoke meant
The shooting of a gun of smoke.

Oh, if the eye could only see
Only other eyes,

And the voice could only smell
The smell of the dead.

THIS MORNING I FOOLED A BUTTERFLY

It was not real, finding an unmarked envelope of old seeds left by dead Dad
It was not real, finding them acting as a place-marker in one of the
armaments catalogues of the electronics industry for which he worked
It was not real, that there was a place left clear for planting among the weeds
that had ensued in the six weeks since his decease
It was not real that these seeds sprouted
It was not real that that happened after three months, during which I could
hardly find the time to return for a visit to the garden beside which my
mother lived in a cottage
It was not real that they were not tended, but came anyway to maturity
It was not real that, as I sat there in the garden, an insect came (some
damned dumb butterfly) and, proceeding straight to the spot, sat on
the product of all this accident, the issue of so much deflection and
misunderstanding
And sat there on the tangle of unknown yellow and blue flowers, and roses,
for a full fifteen minutes, as if all this were real

ON THE LAWN

Just lie back, keep on and lie back, and something is sure to form
Even during the past two hours, while reading, twenty clouds have probably
come together to form a big camel
So, disharmonious pieces of all time are apt to fall together
To form a single contiguous carpet. Here it will be convenient to walk and
run. In the winter slide, in the summer sit, preferably perhaps
somewhat as if at a café.
None of the pieces needs much of a push.
One does not arrange them as one might arrange gunboat formations in a
harbor
Or grapes in an arbor!
Overhead now:
Is that a camel?
An enormous white bee?
An umbrella stand?
A fan, with dark lashes and red lips at the lace edge, looking
over?
A storm?
A foot, poised for the next step forever?

PASSING THROUGH TROY

Get the children of America out of Troy, New York! The awnings hang
    slackly from the doorways in that city
And sooner than usual every young sweetie feels the skin wrinkle
And soft eyes grow smudged as glass on the town hall clock.
As for the young gentlemen of Troy
All they do is sit on curbstones and spit on Greyhound busses, like the one
    I'm riding on, back to New York City.
O cities of the universe
You are not improving anybody much
Except maybe, in some few of you, in the sections that are ritziest,
And what child can afford to live in them after twenty; or return to them,
    unless really rolling in it, after perhaps age forty
Fifth Avenue I love you—but when will I live on you again? Seven more years
    must be waited;
By the time I can cross 67th street once more, and once again enter Central
    Park Zoo conveniently
No doubt my favorite raccoon will be dead.

In the playgrounds of Troy, New York
They have no monkey bars, but things like Lincoln Logs in cast iron
When they grow a garden in Troy, New York, it isn't cultivated, it's invented
Each leaf is a tiny can or a small nail file
The city fathers probably think that the arrangement of gas tanks, barbed-
    wire topped fences, and offensive oil-drums that surround the town,
    and constitute the suburb through which we are now passing
Is some kind of an arboretum.
That's just about enough about you now, Troy, New York

O children of the universe (who live in Troy, New York)
The mind moves on
We have just scratched the surface of the problem
And soon I will be out of the suburbs, even, of Troy, New York

But children of the universe (and of Troy, New York)
I make this suggestion: that the ugliness of Troy, New York, may be
transcended
Move out
But move out to schools and communities located in the countryside on the
East Coast for example and become architects in more beautiful
surroundings
Then come back, and for all people
Build more ritzy districts

So that the mind may hum with unearthly earthly beauty, which after all is
only the beauty of materials
May you begin with the specific:
The creation and maintenance of cities we can stand to stay in—
All the way from Troy, New York, to places in Georgia, like Athens

THE HIGH

1.

Everything is coming down, except that whenever something drops
It meets something on the way up, rising,
So that the air resembles two-way streets whose sidewalks have converged and pedestrians been mingled
Hello, hello, say the shoes to the eye
Hello says the short insect's lower nether foot to the rainbow arc
Hi there says the hog swill flung from the pail at the back door;
Greetings answers my edition of Plato, from the windowsill,
Also I believe I hear greetings being exchanged at this very moment between the highest human accomplishments of all time and the 37 cents the 42nd Street businessman actually ended up by swindling from me after 45 minutes of hassles,
And even between the writings so many of us, including me, once executed free for *The Village Voice*, earnest newspaper consisting about 75% of paid advertisements,
And the famous corporations who supported the 1968 "Festival of the Avant-Garde" (organized by Charlotte Moorman) for reasons unclear, but in a relationship which the same thriving "underground," "liberal" periodical says it finds "suspicious"

2.

There is a theatre opened up in Midtown or in my mind, unadvertised, secret and sacred
"The Little Theatre Just Off Michael Benedikt's Head," it is called
And on stage those ever popular favorites are entering, the lady saints, in long white robes
Then they throw these long white robes aside to reveal bikinis, perforated well, by Rudi Gernreich
And they stride slowly and gracefully all over the stage only pausing occasionally to bump and to grind,
Dance St. Theresa St. Barbara St. Anne and St. Charlotte

Not to mention the rest of you whose names I have forgotten, or which I
never knew
Dance—or else if you can't dance, just jump about a bit, jump up and down,
For the horns of prophets are being raised, entirely electric
For the conch shells of shamans are replaced
With chords in sequences mostly parallel to C, E, and G
And the featured attraction is the Angel of Consciousness
Bust 42", hips 44", waist 28"

THE SKY

After all this experience the sky must feel the vast potential weight
Some of the birds look lighter than usual but consider the seagull lying
there now in a ditch at the water's edge, like an old rock
When the sky sees the flamingo en route it backs off in horror, especially at
the clumsy ones
It will not even stay in the same room as the ostrich
While hummingbirds fall with a thud
And flies and mosquitoes descend and resemble the overtones of clashing
cymbals on an oscilloscope

That is why the sky goes around dropping airliners all the time:
The sky is tired
It has looked at the Boeing 747 Jet on numerous occasions and said "Enough
is enough, I can hardly go on any more—but of course I must"
This is to say that it is less like an apprentice serving maid innocently
dropping dishes in a Bavarian Alp
Than it is like an ancient faithful servant with an annoyed look, shaking
drops of piss from a pervert's favorite mackintosh

This is why I would like to present to this august gathering of all the
dignified people on earth
A concrete proposal:
Everything must become lighter
All phenomena of flora and fauna
When I reach for my cigarette lighter, for example (*he reaches for his cigarette
lighter, lying on the podium*)
I want it to fly away before my hand, since my body has created a breeze (*the
cigarette lighter ascends*)
When I am wearing the best clothing money can buy (*he parts his jacket to
exhibit his matching tweed vest*)

I want it to be delicate as the web of the spider, the only creature which in the above circumstances is still able to fly, I might add in passing (*his body lights up, and we can see that he is wearing a transparent vinyl jump suit*)
When I am speaking the most profound thoughts, I want them to be both enchanting and thrilling (*he writes this poem*)
And when these ideas all age, I want to begin to disappear

FOUR PSALMS

In Memory of Henry Rago, 1915–1969

PSALM I

Everybody has one thing about themselves. What thing? Whatever it is, there is only one of them. Everybody is running up a flag on which some Betsy Ross of the soul has embroidered a picture of himself or herself or a graph of his brain or her brain waves with permanent pleats
To come out, it is necessary to select out all other things.
Nevertheless our atoms are entangled, our flesh is similar, also our joy and our pain are the same, and this inclines me to gentleness.
Besides that, I carry the flag of the salamander, the leaf, and the newt
In my pocket, where the Polaroid photo my mother made of me used to be, I carry a picture of empty space, and of the water's edge

PSALM II

Nothing can be fitted into the past once it is over. No future act can be committed there, or inserted.
To be renewed, even the future has to wait around until more of the present arrives. This is also to say that nothing that will happen in the future can be made to have taken place previously
What is the present supposed to do during all this—sit around counting the grains of sand in an hourglass? Lie around playing Parcheesi? Indulge in games of chance?
Yes.
Past time is like a filled pyramid, while the future is like an apartment on Fifth Avenue in New York City, six rooms, at $200 a month, with doorman; or one on Riverside Drive with the same attractive features for $150; or one in the East Village for $100, or one on Canal street for $50.
That is to say, both are impenetrable realms, only scarcely to be imagined.
How was the world ruled before creation? How will it be ruled after completion? At any rate, not by as pure a poetry as this

PSALM III

Everything is something. Everything that is taking place today has a
completely predictable fate:
Everything, eventually, is going to become History.
Even this meeting, even the very first time you read or hear this poem
Is going (in its small way) to become monumental
Gaining the grandeur that time sheds on events, its proportion, its
dimension, its particular light
This light is the definitive gleam on every circumstance,
The one that makes the lump a monument.
Even if the event seemed meaningless or boring
Hasn't it eventually begun to cast a shadow?
Everything is a big dark something that raises up its huge bulk from the
memorable New Jersey meadows, visible across the river.
With a vague sense of outrage and objection
All will swear, after leading any given life, that it has actually been lived

PSALM IV

Nothing works. The gesture you made to say "go ahead boys, up and at 'em"
catches in the wind, carries you back to the beachhead
A valentine you sent to a lace-loving lady gets delivered to her dog, who eats
it, without reading it,
An octopus you ordered from the South Seas arrives without any arms; and
three weeks later, its little suction cups arrive in a separate crate. You
throw it out, thinking it represents all the buttons you've lost on your
shirts since the age of twelve. You imagine someone has prankishly
returned them to you just at the moment you've given up detailed
clothing, switching to wearing burnooses—
Nothing works. The mind is manufacturing infinite and irrelevant amounts.
The world awaits the invention of the conceptual wheel

LET ME OUT

Let me out! Let me out! I wasn't made to pour old onion soup down the
toilet, I wasn't made to suffer from this dreadful cold
And the boy from the grocery store who is wearing this big cowboy hat and
the fringed shirt and pedaling the bicycle with the big basket for food
is saying, look! my soul is beautiful, too
Oh William Wordsworth and the other 19th century poets from whose dear
Romanticism I first drew hints
You have hinted me very well beyond myself
And now when I write poetry I don't know what I am saying any more, only
what I'm doing
I even noticed that my loves weren't what they should be, thanks a lot,
thanks a lot
Although surely all ladies with nice waists tiny tits and exquisite globèd
asses shall continue to be superb
Let me out! I want to fly without having to stop at the airline terminals
I want to say farewell forever even to the departure points of LaGuardia and
Kennedy airports in New York
No, no explicators; that doesn't mean I'd prefer to use Newark airport, after
all dangerous Leroi Jones lives in Newark
Leroi, Leroi, do you want me to come to your neighborhood in Newark; if
you don't, I won't
Leroi, do you remember the time you crashed that abominable cocktail
party with your old friend, tall, enormous and powerful Charles
Olson?
You both just entered, made three telephone calls (one long distance), and
disappeared in one corner with the plate of hors d'oeuvres (Leroi, that
must have been long ago, before the invention of soul food)
What is Leroi Jones doing in this poem anyway, is he making me immortal
or am I making him immortal; certainly we are large this evening.
Tonight, after supper and an appropriate smoke, my cat started whispering
to me, tales of the stockyards, and the sufferings she knows; for
example the sufferings of beef on the hoof even as it is removed from
the hoof for my supper, by blows on the brain

Oh big blows collapse us all now, it is our own heads we hit, our own arms
It is obvious all this, although it is obvious only temporarily during certain high moments certainly
And I agree with the recent revolutionary who said to me after our talk after our poetry reading: "It is in your poems alone that you speak prose for us"
But also with the host of the abominable cocktail party, whose fate it has been to be bitter forever
When will we see him when will we really see we are the same and who was it anyway that the revolutionary meant when he referred to himself as me, and me, as "you"?
Who is speaking here anyway, can it possibly be me?—What is here and where is "I"?
And how will it be possible to fly with all this great weight of sadness and deliberation
Yes even United Airlines says we are five pounds overweight but as far as I'm concerned I'm 155 pounds overweight
I wonder how it would be to fly now I wonder what it would be like if love were really endlessly desirable possible and present
Let me out. Let me out! Let me out!

THE ESTHETIC FALLACY

Here I'm madly rummaging around in the hall closet thinking it might be
just the right way out in view of this fire at the door
And everybody thinks I'm a secret salesman of flashlights with an
exceptionally fresh approach
Here I can't find the ladder, and am prone to fall into the fatal hole of all fire
escapes
And somebody else tells me that he supposes that this is one more ingenious
plan to advertise the need for plastic parachutes in the home
Oh Coleridge, when you wrote your *Dejection* ode, were you really sitting
there next to your little opium pot covered in chuckles?
Baudelaire, did you actually take a series of sight-seeing tours around Paris
to "get" new material?
Is the patient who lies anesthetized on the operating table in T. S. Eliot's
"The Love Song of J. Alfred Prufrock" really engaging in some new
form of combined indoor and outdoor sport?
We have lingered too long in the house of many means and now our ends
are desperately overdue for condemnation and/or urban renewal.
Send out the repair wagon, wrecking crew, and ambulance now;
Some flesh is real and ill

NAMING THE BABY

Everything is used up, everything is used up, everything is consumed by
History
Thirsty and hungry History, there is no such thing any more as the oasis of
the baby
And we are prevented from starting anything anew or afresh.
Why else dear friends is it so difficult to name this baby today, to identify
this human leaf of Eden, which we pray one day may arise, to join the
tree of people
Why else are all children born wrinkled?

Byron will write many poems, then sink in the sea
Harrison is overly fond of tweed
Vladimir and Otto will compose electronic music
Jean-Luc will make movies
Oswald will shoot the president
Nikita's head is a knob
Rudolph has a red nose, or a concentration camp
Adolf will have an inscrutable fondness for Bavaria
Arthur enjoys round tables
Cedric will smother his uncle
Harvey thinks he's a rabbit
Felix will have a little high-pitched voice and show a marked preference for
milk
Albert will promulgate the theory of relativity
While Phineas will purchase the circus
Estes will appear on television, heading a committee to investigate crime
Cliff will hurt his head by falling off some rocks
While Geronimo will also always be jumping off or out of things with a cry
Phil will develop an excessive fondness for fried finches
Pablo will spend all day up in his room thinking and painting
Rembrandt will always be borrowing money
You'll never catch Babe at home since he'll always be out in lots with a bat
and ball

Clark will fall in love with somebody named "Lois." A second possibility is
starring in movies.
Percy Bysshe will always strike some people as extreme
W. B. will write great verses which suffer initially from soft surfaces
W. H. will write great verses, suffering finally from hard surfaces
T. S. will write great verses, but stop writing them too soon
Mick will wear tight trousers and walk around whispering
Donovan will dunk doughnuts and get drunk
Franklin will have a four-term presidency, and then a cerebral hemorrhage
While Peter, Paul, and Mary will walk around all day eating immaculately
conceived candy bars
Errol will always err
While Michael will accomplish much with regard to expanding our ideas of
structure, despite criticism from the poetically stultified, dumb, and
entrenched

No no don't ask me about possible names for this baby
All I can suggest is that we call him Time; for one thing is certain: surely
Time must be born again

DEFINITIVE THINGS

No, no, they are never the same as their names
Nobody ever fits into his own definition
Who is it regards definitions definitively?
Least of all objects, yes, even those poor helpless things
Knife, you are a butterfly whose wings have been pinned
Pin, you are a knife whose butterfly has been removed
And the sky, which does not agree to stand up when somebody calls upon it
The sky, too, has its windows
See, then, how the word *window* grows troubled, it too closely resembles the
    word *widow*, and that's depressing
I have just said the word *alley* twenty times and find I have forgotten what it
    means: *alley, alley, alley, alley, alley, alley, alley, alley, alley, alley, alley,*
    alley, alley, alley, alley, alley, alley, alley, alley, alley—this blank look on
    our faces is actually a bright beginning
Next is next; I always forgot the meaning of the word *next,* even the first
    time I heard it
Madge, pass me the lung. The lung? That sounds too funny to depend on to
    breathe with! Other words are too short or too long. *Pain* seems too
    abbreviated while *cling* is almost always too short
And if *love* contains within it an appropriate little heart in its *v*
The problem with *death* is that it's too close to *breath*
Food equals *fried* only if you don't happen to be on a diet
Bundle, hunch, flaunt, corpse, lapse, kiss, fiddle, pelt, consume, erode, erotic,
    remake, tape, eyelash
Are 7 one-syllable words and 7 two-syllable words I like
I like all 3 and 4 syllable words for their more complex symmetry
Regarding the names of people, I would *like* to *refer* you to my *poem,*
    "Naming the Baby," *suffice* it to say *here*
Like a hand that does not quite fit a glove
An eye and a contact lens, expectations and the world
Our definitions and meanings never quite overlap
Help help I'm falling off the edge of this page

MIRROR

(Poem-Event for Julian Beck)

I never thought I would start off a poem by saying "I sing"
But here I am nevertheless, about to "sing" something
I'm glad I finally decided to
The question now is what shall it be that I make a beginning by singing
Shall I sing about the pleasure of singing, would that be a waste of a song?
—No, since if I sang it, it starts to be so.
Since the song re-creates the singing, it is serious.
What I sing becomes irrefutable truth in the cornucopia of creation

In all song a really enterprising real estate agent should see lots where
        everything has yet to be established
Earth, rocks, grass and fences; expectations, dreams, and good wishes
        generally for everything
Yet I struggle all the time waste away the day half of what I do is
        contradiction
For example, here's a major theme: I find it barely possible to keep this right
        shirt cuff from protruding from my jacket further than the left. And
        there are other problems even, besides
So that I may say I am perpetually interested for all men in the details of
        improved relations between wrist and sleeve
My good wishes and embraces extend to you all with the same gesture

I know the joy of which we sing must be so,
Here, and in all other things,
And so I sing it

FOR JANE (AND ROGER) BUT CERTAINLY NOT FOR HENRY; OR, *BARBARELLA*

Jane Fonda starring in *Barbarella* I have a secret message for you.
I single out the Jane of *Barbarella* because there have been other Janes and other movies in which you've appeared or starred even in the course of your short Hollywood film career so far—already, you've been cast and shot in many other ways, Jane.
However, the way you appear in this 1968 film is different, Jane.
In this film you appear—eek!—semi-nude most of the time.
And what with all the transparent clothing and peek-a-boo fashion you wear in this daring new Hollywood film
Everybody's saying that it's the degree of nudity in *Barbarella* which makes it so exciting
—Everybody that is except for the people who enjoy the weird science-fiction costumes you wear and there are quite a few of them I mean there are quite a few of both weird sci-fi costumes and people who seem to find the film remarkable because of them. For example, the 3 fashion-design-savvy gay friends with whom I first went to see this film...
—But that's unusual, let's just say that the majority enjoy the semi-nudity.

No, no, that's where they're wrong—like most public truth
That too, is a truth which is far too general; there too, there's a misapprehension to be corrected:
It's not the degree of nudity in *Barbarella* compared to other Hollywood films which distinguishes it, any more than it's the clothing which you threw aside which distinguishes you.
—After all, some day all clothing may go out of fashion, some day society may throw it aside entirely; there could come a time when nudity too, could go out of style; some day nudity both onscreen and offscreen may become so ordinary that everybody will go around mistaking it for just one more form of fashion;
Some day the world may even begin to think of skin as just one more maddeningly intimate form of underwear...

Jane, Jane, this is my secret message for you
Jane, Jane, this is my secret public message for you (and also for your
husband Roger Vadim, who happens to be the director of this film
and who happened previously to be the husband and director of
Brigitte Bardot, whom I also didn't mind too much)
Here in the lobby of this moviehouse having just seen you in *Barbarella* for
the 3rd time in just 2 weeks,
Writing upon this crumpled scrap of paper and standing next to an already
slightly faded movie-poster while using the glass on one side of a
popcorn machine as my desk
I scribble out in ink that's almost invisible because doomed for the
outrageous oblivion of the audience for true poetry here in this world
of impossibly public perception we presently endure

That I too, belong to that Club Of Love, that not-so-secret society totally
enthralled by your good looks
As you stand there in the poster with your perfect hour-glass figure posed
almost in profile,
With both bosoms half-bared and wearing tights and tall boots
And looking vulnerable yet still defiant with your right hand propped on
your right hip and with a sharp knife held in that same hand...

—Which is why Jane, whatever you may do in the future perhaps with this
poster as reminder, fans like me will always remember
Your young daring; and how you looked and the sexy way you moved and
the eager, breathless way you spoke
Even early on, even in your 1968 film *Barbarella*.

TO PERSUADE A LADY

Carpe Diem

True, I have always been happy that all the things that are inside the body
are inside the body and that all things outside the body, are out.
I'm glad to find my lungs on the inside of my chest, for example; if they
were outside, they'd keep getting in the way, those two great incipient
angel wings; besides, it would be messy
I mean, how would it be if you reached out to shake someone's hand and
there, in the palm, were a kidney and a liver complete with spleen?
Can you imagine standing at 5 p.m. in a crowded subway car full of empty
stomachs?
What if a nice, nearsighted old lady were knitting socks and suddenly her
veins fell out? How would she avoid creating a substance full of
strangeness and pain? To the barefoot country boy sitting on the edge
of the bed in the morning opening Aunt Minnie's gift box, the sight of
these socks would be what he'd call "a real eye-opener!"
And what if our voices touched? If our mouths went out, instead of in? If
you were inside of me; or, at least, if I were inside of you?

from

Mole Notes

SOCIAL CONCERNS

Waking, Mole's greatest social concern at present is this large rock. The earth must have rolled around until the mouth of his burrow was directly under it; then it stopped.

THE SANDHOG'S MONOLOGUE

Is it at the center or the edge? Perhaps it's enough that I simply recognize its presence, hanging there in front of my eye like a loose eyelash. But loose eyelashes don't mean much; following a night of regret, or twisting and turning, and elaborate psychic gyrations, it's easy enough to understand awakening and finding oneself a man with tousled eyelashes. But the something was present all the following day; and last night it was also evident. The next morning, the same presence but a different analogy: it was as apparent as a Cuban gunboat steaming up the Potomac toward the Capitol. Curious, I said; but I'm not president, am I? And I rolled over and went back to sleep. Later that same morning, at work, as I was attending to my molar labors, the speck in my eye continued to bother me, prominent now as a tombstone in a teacup. Perhaps I should say what my job is: everybody says I look like an intellectual but actually I'm some kind of sandhog. At the moment I have a project over near the river: I'm trying to dig a tunnel between this city and the promised land, using only my bare hands and feet. Obviously if this something of a presence were real, I'd be among the first to be equipped to remove it. But the days go by and it grows more ungraspable; and as time has gone on, I've become so used to it I've even given up making analogies for it. But it looks enough like an enormous boulder lying on my eye to turn my eye in on itself, and remind me how full of memories I am already. For example, I recall a passage from an astronomy textbook I once read in preparation for my vocation as an astrophysicist. It said, in its exquisitely scientific, professional prose: "When we look out into outer space, the optical evidence is that the earth is situated unchangeably at the center of the Milky Way, the galaxy of which it is a part; and yet it is a physical fact that at this very moment the planet is moving rapidly across space to some other galactic universe. This new universe is located just west of Cygnus the Swan; or, as it is sometimes called, the constellation of the Northern Cross." So is it at the center or the edge?

OF THE DIFFICULTY OF FINDING A FRIEND

Mole tries to find a friend. What is the best way to go about such a thing? A mole figures out an answer for himself. Circling around the underground part of the large rock, he digs a long, long tunnel, and comes up right in the middle of a large garden party in Scarsdale. The conversation is certainly interesting: one man is delivering an impromptu monologue regarding his collection of antique pornographic beer steins, all picturing episodes from the Satyricon, and none weighing less than fifty pounds or liftable without the help of three hands or two friends. A lady dressed in dark furs is whispering to another lady about her new lover, a dynamite manufacturer, and also about a new set of exploding golf clubs she has just secretly given her husband's habitual caddy. Yet another lady is rubbing her legs together and referring, in a way she thinks is wittily detached, to a new TV star everyone calls "The Poison Dirigible." It is around this time that it occurs to Mole that he might not have too much in common with these interesting inhabitants of Scarsdale. He is about to turn around in his tunnel and go back home, using the route beneath the toolshed, when suddenly he thinks of a sure-fire way to start a conversation. A hopeful, friendly smile on his face, he pops up in the middle of a circle of three ladies with plates on their laps. Very politely, he asks: "Would anybody here like to come down sometime and see my worm collection?" Evidently not; suddenly he feels an empty hors d'oeuvres tray whizz past his whiskers; and so not only does he have to withdraw abruptly from his debut in social conversation, but all that night he has to listen to the sound of rakes, hoes, and shovels pounding down on the roof of his home; the sound of spades digging up almost the entire lawn; and the sound of cars backing up with hoses attached to their tailpipes, filling every hole in the ground with carbon monoxide exhaust, while he sits quietly in the tunnel beneath the toolshed, quaking.

HOW A NAVY MAN GOES DOWN

Old soldiers never die.

—General Douglas MacArthur (January 26, 1880–April 5, 1964)

He dreams of being surrounded by rushing sounds—it must be enemy aircraft on the attack. They go soaring around his head and buzz the brain, then one dives into his collar; it comes out through the starched cuff of his shirt. He waves his arms around wildly but one swoops up his pants leg and then comes out his fly that wasn't quite closed. What were the enemy aircraft doing beneath his clothing? Don't worry—they were only scout planes on a reconnaissance mission! Out of a cloud comes an entire squadron, blue as the sky, flying in perfect formation and buzzing like angry hornets: they break formation and one by one dive down and in an instant they've torn the gold braid off his suit jacket and are gone again; then the Navy Man becomes aware of an aircraft carrier off in the distance, firing at his newly polished shoes . . . a scuba diver starts climbing up his left pants leg; he feels a little tug at his waist and notices his belt buckle is opening, but before he can close it up again his pants fall down. Suddenly a blue helicopter is hovering overhead; it lets down four ropes with hooks at the end and, while he is staring down at his pants, they cunningly remove his service cap, as in guerilla warfare; then his regulation Navy hair flies off in the breeze and his false teeth fly out. Another helicopter appears: its four ropes lower to his shoulders, then as far as his wrists; and together, the eight hooks rip off his jacket. In the meantime, a team of underwater demolition experts undo the laces on his boots and pull his socks down; in an instant his new regulation t-shirt is burnt off by airborne flame throwers. "Oh, leave him his shorts at least!" a lady technician's voice calls out from a battleship that is advancing with all its guns firing. But then a squadron of pilots on a suicide mission arrives in the sky; one after another, despite his cries, they peel off from formation and dive their blue aircraft, aircraft blue as the infinite, down his throat; and one hears muffled internal explosions. Well, he's gone down now; but at least as the Navy's only ten-star admiral he had the right to choose his own means of cremation, and to demonstrate that cremation and creation are actually the same. And as his scalp sinks slowly in the West, his devoted men, who are all poets at heart, give him a 22-gun salute—it's the salute reserved for the Navy's only ten-star admirals and their admirers; also, this salute is an honor reserved especially for distinguished fortune tellers, retiring jockeys, and female impersonators.

THE ANGELS; OR, GOD'S EYEBALL

The angels, the conventional angels of history, are coming to turn in their wings—a long line of identical pilgrims winds out of the warehouse where they are supposed to turn them in; the line stretches out in a straight line as far as that cliff over there in the distance; then the angel line comes down at an angle from the air, after slicing off from space. It's true that all these beatings of wings give the impression of taking off, but actually they're the sounds of vast numbers of seraphim wings hovering and landing for the last time. Inside the warehouse, despite the obvious fact that this turn-in represents a gesture of considerable philosophical gravity, feathers fill the air, and there is an atmosphere like that of a pillow fight in a dormitory for very young girls. After processing, the angels come out the other side of the warehouse (a structure which is best described by saying that it resembles God's eyeball); some are laughing and joking as if relieved, making supercilious remarks about nature and mankind and chatting casually about life in the fourth dimension where they hear they are going to be shipped to live from now on. The rest seem deflated and two-dimensional: they frown, look pale, carry attaché cases, pursue careers in sales, act seriously, walk like mechanical men and women, and have keys coming out of their backs. Everybody seems slightly uncomfortable about these suits of new clothing they have been given to wear; and even now, so soon, they seem puzzled when they find the single long feather which has been placed in each suit for a souvenir. Also, as a second souvenir, everybody gets an indescribably beautiful and exciting plastic ashtray which is an exact replica in miniature of the warehouse; stamped on it in the silvery lettering angels are supposed to like are the words "God's Eyeball," together with the date of the present year.

THE NEW CHRIST

The lady eight months pregnant entered the room in which everyone was carrying on in a gay way. Despite the fact that the room was very crowded with carousers and merrymakers, the bump of her unborn baby so altered the center of gravity in the party, that a wallflower who happened to be poised on the edge of the ledge ready to jump off because she had not mastered the art of conversation, and who was placing all her hope in her ability to fly, was sucked back into the room and landed on the lap of *some very famous former movie star!*

ON PAINTING THE BATHROOM WINDOW

I'm trying to get something done for a change: I'm trying to get away from this tattered stack of manuscripts. Enough concepts! What I want to do now is some household task, beginning by repainting the entire house, starting with the battered old window above the bathroom sink. One coat covers up all the old paint; but whenever I reach down with my brush to touch up the knife slashes and other broken places in the paint where the original wood is still showing, the paint is instantly absorbed into the wood. It's something about "fibre"—each time I paint over "fibre," the wood starts to drink up my paint. My father the carpenter used to say that the wood was "thirsty"; and that, to satisfy its thirst, it needed a drink of paint resin. That's why I give the wood a second coat, then a third coat; and each time, while I'm waiting around between the coats for the thirsty wood to finish, I make myself a little something to sip, too. And sometimes I come back in time to see the original wood finishing up its drink—no longer acting like exhausted wood in an old family bathroom, and I can see it satisfying its thirst like an antelope with lowered head, leaning over some pool in a clearing, gratefully drinking, sip after silent sip.

THE JOURNEY ACROSS YOUR THIGH

At last! The greatest of all explorations on earth! Our ten intrepid travelers set out across the vast expanse by traversing the narrowest section of the promontory. Confident, cheerful, chatting, they are moving spiritedly, and breathing easily despite the fact that they are heavily loaded down with jewels, rings, and other token trinkets in case of chance encounters with hostile or greedy natives. Now they pass out of sight over the distant, enormous horizon; and there is silence, except for an occasional ecstatic cry. But what *can* be going on now behind those hills? All you can hear all of a sudden is a lot of panting and hoarse and desperate breathing! Then there is a series of outraged gasps; and then the sound of struggle! Finally the leader of the expedition reappears. It's an eye, crawling in on all fours! "What happened?" we anxiously enquire; but all it can do is choke out a few words of feverish explanation through parched lips. "This eye's throat is dry," someone says; "—it's obviously because its canteen of tears has been emptied." As for the eye itself, it has just fainted. Carefully, swaddled in its eyelid, we carry the exhausted eyeball back to safety, only to see it awake a few hours later in this apparent terminal which evidently it does not yet realize is only the base camp from which an entirely new set of still more perilous expeditions are about to set out.

ESTHETIC NUPTIALS

I invited our favorite famous writer, who happens to be a distant friend, to our wedding. To celebrate, he gets high and cuts up the manuscript of one of his most famous love poems, using a paper punch; then he throws it all over us in our hotel room, like confetti. And everybody considers us just one more nice normal average couple when I tell them that we spent the first night of our love in a motel room crawling around on our hands and knees.

PHYSICAL LOVE

(1) Everybody knows that, whenever true lovers encounter, the last thing it is, is mechanical. Nothing is a thing. It is so direct, so physical, the pressure is so specific, that when one part of one lover rubs against the other, if it rubs with any strength, the other part actually falls off. It falls to the floor; and among true lovers, nobody moves to sweep it underneath the rug. Delicate, radiant, and palpitating, as the relationship continues, more and more pieces come to lie there beneath the rug. Also, they lie there beneath tables, chairs, and (especially) couches in the doctor's waiting room. Oh, as everybody knows, all true lovers are only too happy to accept making love in littered rooms! (2) That must be why all true lovers will always notice—not because of lechery, but because of all the pieces falling off—how increasingly rounded any other lover seems. (3) But is there no distinction then between the most delicate abrasions, irritations, and touching; and hitting something?—Is all this making love just one more version of beating somebody up, of slapping somebody in the face, or cutting off parts of each other's bodies with knives? (4) I myself have often felt whittled to approximately the size of a pair of tennis balls or handballs. (5) At least, in any case, all true lovers must accept the fact that when they leave each other for good, they will not be able to leave each other the same as when they found them.

PORTABLE WAR

(1) There are people who are pressing to end this war, and Mole considers himself one of them, having even by adolescence spent more than his share of time digging for peace; then later, actually digging peace, revising political manuals to include serious discussions of the process of Molarization, etc. Still, he tries not to forget that the pleasure he has begun to take in these activities ought not to amount to a delight in struggle for struggle's sake, or effort for effort's sake, those contemporary, immoral, evil, and decadent versions of Art for Art's sake. (2) For a mole, the sole struggle becomes to contradict faith in pain; he becomes convinced that, in war and out, hell on earth consists of depending for one's bliss purely on the reactions of those in opposition to one's position. (3) It becomes clear to a mole: there are people who say they are pressing to end the war, but whose pleasure in conflict suggests that they are in fact The War, have always been The War, will always be The War.

OF HOLES

(1) Bad night. Harder even to sleep than to think. Entire body clenched like teeth, omitting no finger, cell, or nail. At least, if these teeth were smiling . . . but no, this is a genuine grimace. It's the fault of the dark, it's the fault of the dark!—suddenly it fails to resemble one big single nice enormous nothingness, but instead resembles an endless series of emptinesses laid out end to end. Beside the bed, the holes of a harmonica look like the famous bottomless pits of the Mindanao Deep, in the Philippines. Nor, looking at the pores in your nose, are we spared the sight of the Black Hole of Calcutta. Either everything has now become empty, or else nothing needs to be filled, since everything here is crowded solid with these holes, vacuums, and tunnel-like spaces. (2) I fall asleep counting the edges of the emptiness as if they were sounds from the bell around the necks of the sheep I'm supposed to be counting. So this is supposed to be relaxing, this is supposed to put people to sleep? Oh, that's funny, very funny—notwithstanding the fact that I'm lying here frowning from head to foot. (3) And here, in the morning, beside the bed, is this sheet of paper covered with words, an effort no doubt to fill the empty spaces with some kind of sound. But if this is only a compromise vote for noise, there must be a better way; already I'm thinking that another way of voting would be to go out to the middle of the forest to invent a ballot box by shouting at the top of one's lungs into a hollow tree.

A HOPE CHEST IN REVERSE

For the sake of his continued "development" he was always shedding a new skin. Finally he had a chest full of them, a sort of hope chest in reverse. So in order to convince everyone of his continuing progress he held a celebration. At the party he came out wearing all these ancient diaphanous rags—of course he was trying to convince everyone of his philosophical advancement, but all he looked like was someone who had cut his entire body badly while shaving and who had covered himself with tissue paper from head to foot to stanch the flow of blood. His best friend, who happened to be present (and who also was later canonized for being a saint), said something kindly: he said he "resembled a pile of litter whose basket had been removed." His friend the Saint's girl-friend also cheered him up when she said that with his odd old garb and extensive and theatrical gestures of farewell, he kept reminding her of the strips of paper they fasten in festoons to the vents of air-conditioners in Chinese restaurants in the summer to assure the patrons of the presence of fresh air.

CHRISTMAS ON EARTH AND OTHER VACATIONS WITH PAY

(1) Their famous curious position: almost everybody knows it; but of course almost nobody believes it. What they insist on is that it is better to give than to receive; and, by implication, that the best blessings are the ones denied, and by extension, that to reject and to donate are identical. They dream all their lives of such abandoned richness! Naturally, this subjects their sense of personal worth to the most outrageous inflation. Therefore, it is useful to the unprejudiced observer to consider whether these gifts they imagine they have denied were actually intended for them in the first place; also, whether if—should they eventually receive them—it will simply be because there was no one else around to give them to at the time. And if the latter happens to be true, why couldn't they have been asked to take these gifts into at least temporary safekeeping until the advent of the rightful owner? Couldn't they have been trusted? (2) In any case, because of their famous curious positions, it must be that Christmas on Earth is here. The Children and I spend all day singing in the streets, making generous gestures along Fifth Avenue, and looking for the poor there with magnifying glasses. Also, all of us are leaning forward slightly, as if expecting something. But what is It? All we know for sure is that it is "gifts"; and that they must be coming from someplace else than *this*. (3) Yet why, every year so far, on the night after Christmas, do I have this vision of God getting up in the middle of the night, going to the bathroom, and flinching at finding the remains of all this tinsel on his nose? (4) And as for our Eastertime: it is an Interruption to the Resurrection. Here comes our old friend the Easter Bunny now; he is covered in black synthetic polyester fur, carrying two submarine guns, and occasionally taking target practice by firing into the air from the hip.

IN THE HOSPITAL

So we see the landscape of being alive at last! At last, after a long time of traveling we've arrived here, in the middle of the night, where we can really feel completely abandoned! Here anything visible turns out to be rocks. All there are, are these definite impressions, all so clear-cut that the shapes of the language needed to describe them threaten to cut off little pieces of the tongue, the lips, the chin, nose, hands, feet, and other organs. The subjects for which there are ideas, and the ideas for which there are subjects, all suggest that even in case of the most extreme suffering or torture, nobody ought to look for sympathy. Even down at the Hospital, on one of the brand-new deathbeds they have there—the ones with the built-in television sets—you might have to hold your own hand. And as for daily life, the way things are now, it is clear that the only things people feel like hearing about less than your illnesses are your inconveniences. To heal the pain one depends on having enough medicine; for a complete cure, one waits for time and nothing else. Earlier expectations, the ones you had as an innocent invalid individual, were probably impossible anyway; didn't they come from theorists whose beliefs were celebrated to the degree that they were either unbelievable or could not be realized? Now, at last, you yourself are responsible for whatever reverie you have left. And all you dream of now is a hand on your forehead during light fevers, the fevers which have always been your firmest impressions, the kind of fever you had as a child and which sent your parents back and forth down the hall to your bedroom on tiptoe all night. But besides this hand, you dream of one other thing: when you are well and running, an arm to keep you from falling. Even the metal one, with silver fingernails, which took such good care of you when you were asleep at the dentist. But on waking, as I do now at the end of this, defend yourself from memory; O Memory, when you and I were alone, and cried out in real or imagined pain, don't remind me now, when I feel like this, of a mother who never believed in weaknesses either, of the midnight angers of the father.

EMBODIMENT OF EMBEDDEDNESS

What if you thought that the best way to cross a wall was to systematically destroy everything on the side where you are, and opposite to where you wanted to be? And what if, after a while, you felt you ought to be all the way through, since nothing at all was left anymore on your side; but what if when you lifted your head you found that you were not only still in transit, but embedded halfway, stuck in the wall? That red overhead would not be the color of a new sky, then, but rather the tint of brick; and you are not seeing a new world, but the thickness in which you are sunken, in cross-section. In effect, you are buried alive! You cry out in a characteristic manner: "So this is how a white corpuscle must feel when improperly lodged in an inappropriate artery!" Some doctors are going by then; to them you cry out that you are engaged in useful and productive medical research. But when they hear voices coming out of the wall, the doctors go off to the doctor's, to get their heads examined. And to the left and right, despite the fact that you are stuck head first, you hear the clanging of gates; the shuffling footsteps of people going in and out; or else, worse, the sound of open gates simply swinging back and forth, opening, in the wind.

UNDERSTANDING; OR, A MUCH BETTER PLACE FOR THE SAME PRICE

At last, some ultimate philosophical questions! (1) Is there any greater human humiliation than dining in the worst corner snack bar on the Upper West Side—the Remeldia Luncheonette at Broadway and 69th Street—and understanding that it is awful as you go there, but knowing also that you *have* to go there, because you don't have the cash to dine elsewhere? (2) Or is it a greater human humiliation to eat at the most terrible corner snack bar on the Upper West Side without at all understanding how absolutely awful it is in the first place? (3) And is it better or worse to be indifferent to the whole thing, and not even to care about going around the corner to the Ace Luncheonette, which you recall from past days, and which you *know* is really a much better place for the same price.

THE NIGHT OF THE FOOT

In exorcism of my foot ill, 9/70, and in memory of lost explorers and an astronaut

It is very dark tonight inside the foot. This is logical enough: isn't it one of the deepest regions of the body? It is so shadowy here that traveling through like this we can see only the light-colored objects:—the good bones moving around slowly, like travelers at half-fare, dignified, with shabby baggage; bones, but bad ones, slipping off like maniacs escaping from a train; bones still intact, but dipped in the deepest bitterness of foot blood; little yearning and loving bones signaling to hidden magnetic partners opposite them in nearby feet, constantly sliding back and forth so close yet so far away; bones dislocated, misplaced in the heel, fallen down great heights from the leg, lying for a long time broken at the bottom of the body like a fallen mountain climber; loose bones rattling around the ankle the way coins for a non-existent false cause rattle around a collection can in sophisticated downtown "cinema"; mysteriously roving gypsy bones, jingling palpably as they roam back and forth from one end of the foot to the other; bones that travel in fragments, like a quarreling family on the money-saving Family Plan, wandering disconsolately over the famous and picturesque natural arch bridge; and there are bones that keep on detaching themselves with suspicious casualness, wandering like sailors along 43rd Street between Eight Avenue and Broadway in New York City; and also there are veins; veins waiting for the Jules Verne, the Captains Nemo and Ahab, the Edgar Allan Poe, the Amelia Earhart, the Richard Halliburton, the Arthur Gordon Pym, the Virgil Grissom of bones, just to rupture.

from

Night Cries

EXPLANATION OF THE DARK

Blackest night: a pack of animals is coming down the street, hair by hair! Where are they going to? You'll never know until you feel the fuzz brush up against your throat—you'll find out from fangs; damp paws, dear child, will elucidate you

A GIFT

It's a specially designed pistol for committing suicide, with a muzzle at one end and on the other a bottle-opener, in case you should decide to drink yourself to death.

THE MEAT EPITAPH

This is what it was: Sometime in the recent but until now unrecorded past, it was decided by cattle ranchers that since people were increasingly insistent that "you are what you eat," all cattle on the way to market were to be marked with brief descriptive tags noting the favorite food of each beast, and how much each ate of it. This, it was felt, would both delight the diner and comfort the consumer: people would be able to tell exactly what kind of flavor and texture beef they were purchasing beforehand, and always secure exactly the kind of product most likely to delight their taste. (It was something a little like our present-day system of catering to preferences for light and dark meat in chicken.) The system set up seemed ideally efficient: first, they attached the tag to each beast on its last day on the ranch, just before the two or three days required for shipment to the slaughterhouse—during which travel time the animal customarily doesn't eat anything, anyway. Once at the slaughterhouse, they carefully removed the tags; and during the slaughtering, duplicated the so-called "parent tag" numerous times, preparing perhaps hundreds of tiny tags for each animal. Directly after, at the packing plant, these were affixed to the proper parts, each section of each animal being separately and appropriately tagged, each as if with an epitaph. But something went wrong with this means of augmenting the diner's delight and of comforting the consumer. At first, quite predictably, the tags came out reading things like "Much grass, a little moss, medium grain" and "Much grass, much grain, generally ate a lot." And this, as one might expect, proved a great pleasure to the consumer. But then tags began coming through reading things like "A little grass, small grain, many diverse scraps from our table": And "She was our favorite, gave her all we had to give"; and there was one (featured at dinnertime one evening on national television news) saying, "Goodbye, Blackie Lamb, sorry you had to grow up—we'll miss you." Gradually, despite its efficiency, this system somehow ceased to delight the diner and comfort the consumer. And this is how the practice of the meat epitaph began to become generally neglected during the course of time, and how people came to eat their meat, as they generally do today, partially or wholly blindfolded.

THE TASTE FOR ALL THINGS FORMAL

(1) "I ask you: is there one man in the world who doesn't long every now and then for that feeling of formality, that sense of artifice, that certain feeling of neatness and security which only a tuxedo jacket can really provide, surrounding its wearer so snugly with its square-cut shape, its elaborately decorated box-cut cuffs, and above all and before all its glossy, brilliantly shining lapels?" I was lying in bed reading the ads for fancy evening dress, or (as they termed it in the ads beside the social notes column in *The Daily News*), "What every man needs to truly experience that certain feeling of 'stepping out'"; yet still, somehow, I wasn't completely convinced. On the other hand, I did have to admit that I myself that night wished I had a way of experiencing that certain feeling of "stepping out" instead of lying here like a shut-in, envying the gay formal times people always have in their tuxedos. But then, out of one corner of my eye, I saw it: my brand new armoire. It was true that all it contained were things like buckskin jackets, beads and blue jeans, and tweeds baggy with "that certain lived-in look," all crammed in together and half-falling-off their hangers; but still, there was no mistaking it: the armoire itself was impeccably formal with its tall, rectangular outlines, its elaborate yet symmetrical trim around the sides, and the polished mirrors to the left and right of the center door. So, to achieve that certain feeling of "formally stepping out," I stood up and stepped into the armoire, closing the door after me; and there I spent the entire night having a gay, formal evening. (2) The following morning, while she was dusting around the room, the cleaning lady found me. "What are you doing in there, Sir?" she asked, peering through the keyhole. "Isn't it obvious?—I've been stepping out," I explained. "Did you have a good time, Sir?" she asked, eagerly scanning the interior for noisemakers or perhaps the remnants of a party hat. "Of course I did," I replied; and, anxious to continue to my new-found role of impeccable formal partygoer and general *bon vivant*, I gallantly appended an invitation: "How would you like to come along with me next time?" "Certainly, Sir," she said, "but I have nothing to wear." "Don't worry about that, my dear," I said, gesturing toward the opposite side of the room. (3) And so we began a round of gay formal outings with our first date, stepping out in the finest and most proper manner—me, so debonair there in the armoire; she, the belle of the ball over there in the corner, wrapped up in my freshly ironed chintz curtains, with the valance pleats folded flat over her face.

A FACE IN THE TRASH

(1) I took the top off the trash can outside my bachelor apartment and what should I see there amidst the usual beer cans, peanut shells, and fat scraps; citrus-fruit rinds and old poetry textbooks, and the many other anonymous and almost unidentifiable slimes such pails are apt to contain, but a woman's face made entirely out of garbage. And all at once, she smiled at me!—Or were those teeth just a series of overly alive-looking old olive pits? But believe me, everything was perfectly under control. Yes, when our gossipy and scandal-mongering neighbors saw me, lid in hand, leaning over yesterday's garbage, transfixed and looking as if I were about to fall in, everything was perfectly under control, because everything was still perfectly above-board between us. (2) But then, as it always does, it happened. Suddenly the woman of my dreams started becoming "forward," began leering instead of smiling, hinting the usual things about "a quick smooch where nobody else can see," her suggestive manner obviously calling for the all-too-usual "fast little visit to my place, baby." But still, everything remained perfectly under control because, to show how firmly I rejected her indecent proposals, I said goodnight and slammed the door to her apartment right smack in her face! (3) Tomorrow, of course, just for the sake of decency and politeness, I'll make it up to her: I'll do it by composing a long note of apology, crumpling it up, and throwing it away just as soon as I finish writing it. Then I'll make it up to her some more by phoning the florist's and ordering a dozen roses to be delivered directly to the garbage pail outside my home. (4) Then I'll really be able to feel once more that things are still rational and perfectly under control, just as perfectly under control as ever.

THE MELANCHOLY MORALIST

Am I really supposed to stay here with the rest of these people making the usual surreptitious motions, tentative gestures, and shifting around guiltily from foot to foot? Because I can feel that there is obviously not going to be enough room to move in this room. To scratch the top of my head I have to go slipping my arm around the side of my head in a guilty way, as if it were a journey by Rolls-Royce around a bend in a mountain road in the poverty region, all the while praying that nobody accuses the hollow of my armpit of causing competition with a shut-down coal mine. Just so, I am amply assured that whenever I reach up to scratch my nose, a boxcar falls over in Alabama, as does a beer can in the Alhambra. And should I lower my eyelashes to express the requisite embarrassment, a bird's nest falls out of the tree in a field beside the farm. According to these definitions, I'll have to black out both my eyes in order to be able to say I see! And if I decide to deeply inhale, the tender finger of the saintly child beside me here, the one giving me the long lecture on delicacy, holding me by the lapel with one hand, and poking me in the chest with the other, becomes blunted. Also, inhaling risks bursting the stained glass windows in this beautiful room they have locked us all in. The Poetry Library would fall! The orphanage will be eaten up by an ogre! And to think, I originally came here to this place because I heard it was the ideal place to go if you wanted to open a career in modern dance.

THE DISAPPOINTED PHILANTHROPIST

How do you feel, you who yearned half your life for endless friends, but discover that all you've ended up with is a succession of clever operators? Well-schooled in charitable ways at only the most privileged of academies, how could you have realized that when you said your first friendly hello to any stranger, your voice would inevitably be tape-recorded, the sound amplified and stored away for eventual use in shattering eggshells among the indigent egg-suckers of Peru; that during any appearance in public the slightest stray breeze of your celebrated sympathetic breath would be compressed for use in running a waterwheel set up horizontally by some local government idiot in the very midst of the provinces of Sand; that should you even go so far as to smile your gold-toothed smile at a passing stranger, the second time around he was apt to return with a jewelry-appraiser disguised as a desert saint; or that when you held out your hand to the professional beggar, he would invariably place it palm down on a butcher's scale? Oh, so very well-trained in the care and feeding of all the would-be recipients of anything they can lay their hands on whatsoever, how did you feel the first time you noticed that, since you were said to weep so often with concern, the back door of your modest home had become completely surrounded by a series of secret souvenir stands selling tears?

THE ADVENTURES OF RESENTMENT

Resentment, you remember—since somebody told you once—spreads like a stain. But somehow, now it's also a point of light in the brain, a train coming toward you down a long tunnel. It pulls up at the little station and you get on. Out of the tunnel, beyond the station, you ride ten thousand miles. Out in the light you immediately become the world's most celebrated traveler. Little children gather by the railway line to see you pass by. For miles around, the multitude grows grudgingly aware of your integrity. Chugging along, sitting in the window, your tongue out, making faces, and giving everybody The Finger, you become a sight yourself; you grow almost as popular as Lincoln's coffin. Rounds of applause, stompings of feet at crossroads! Finally, contracts arrive; gifts, grants, awards, offers to appear in public or on educational TV! You even begin to look forward to further adventures. That's exactly when, for some reason, the point of light begins to pull slowly away, back down the track. You find yourself standing in some stupefying station in Idaho with all the home folks, eyes dull, a blank look on your face, loving everything and finally cleansed of resentment.

LIVING WITH ADVERSITY

There are some mountains you can't move. Moreover, not only that, but you will find yourself under severe pressure to sit there at their feet, lying around for half your life, like some sweet boy or girl scout, saying how happy you are, and exclaiming about how good it is to simply experience such scenic beauty, and at such great length. After all, haven't you been explicitly notified that generations upon generations of calendar-makers have been literally depending upon these distant romantic views for their support?—So that even if you decide to climb them, you know you shouldn't, since it might throw a great many people out of work. Every step would have to be an apology. Every step a regret. Finally, once they know you know the feelings expected of you—what great guilt—they hand you the spiked hiking shoes. It's kind of these people; you know you're supposed to feel, except that you notice that instead of being on the outside of this shoe, facing down, the spikes have been placed on the inside of the shoe, facing up—a simple mistake, you know you will have to hasten to reassure them. That's when you learn that all the local artisans and shoemakers, too, are rumored to be terribly upset about their little error; and so you have to visit their basements to reassure them that you forgive them, too, and to apologize for causing them upset, before you start to climb. Still, slowly, you ascend.

THE VOYAGE OF SELF-DISCOVERY

It's the voyage of self-discovery: it started out with enormous sails, a drunken captain, and a bosun going toot-toot. Now, when you think you hear them piping you to quarters, it usually turns out to be a reference to a heavy smoker who is about to receive interest at the bank. So now the ship sits upon this bank, fifteen feet above sea level, dripping ooze from all her portholes. It seems a pleasant enough little bay, however, and the captain, who has just discovered after the disaster that he is still an incurable optimist, wonders if, given enough time and money, the old hulk might not be converted from a former four-masted schooner to a large barge for inland waterway travel, or even, just possibly, a houseboat.

DISCOURAGING EVENING

Hiccupping sounds in the night—then pretty soon the smell of cat vomit beneath the bed where my life's companion and I are lying. One of us ought to get up and clean it up, but both of us are pretending not to hear. Neither of us moves even when the odor suffuses the air. And it's not that we were up much late last night; it's not that we've been fucking; we haven't been anything, much. It's just that we're both too plain lazy to move. Also, the thing is that we really can't get too upset about the cat vomiting; we're so sick of ourselves, and each other. We tuck our two heads under our arms and under our two pillows and await shit to fall from the ceiling, anything.

THE PILLS

Midnight—An alternative way of looking at it: All around the globe, whenever and wherever the clock strikes midnight, billions and billions of the prescription and non-prescription sleeping pills which restless, stressed-out people worldwide take about an hour before bedtime are starting to dissolve in billions and billions of stomachs. Now at last, without resorting to any of our usual, overblown social rhetoric—and in fact, without any kind of sentimentality whatsoever—we well-intentioned people around the globe can truly claim that we belong to a world of "Brothers and Sisters Beneath The Skin."

*

He tossed and turned so that when he tried to catch up on lost sleep in the late afternoon, just before dinnertime, his wife used to secretly affix a salad bowl to his backbone, as he lay there. Russian dressing was his specialty.

*

We use the phrase "going to sleep" because sleep really *is* a place to go to; we spend all day arriving there, driving hard down the highways of staying awake, under the underpasses and across the shortcuts; and we have to travel far, too, speeding through our lives at the rate of 16 hours per day.

*

Looking for cool places on a pillow on a summer night—No Columbus ever set out on a more difficult mission, or a more perilous one, we have come to recognize; consider our fate, for example, lying here completely upsidedown, having fallen out of bed, with our feet in the air.

THE AWARDS OF WATER

At first it seemed as if it were the morning coffee again, overflowing in the percolator with the usual loud hiss; but then, when I reached the kitchen, I saw that the brown stain on the white stove was in the form of a "splash," which is to say a circle with fringed edges, and that it was actually only another form of water setting its seal of approval on solids. Do raindrops act any differently, I wondered; do they approve, too, with their pure, glueless, transparent stickers? Even now, as the morning coffee is brewing, we can be sure that the dew is descending in all directions to award billions of blue ribbons to everything firm; that the rushing of rivers is like the roar of applause; and that the only reason why we do not regard the Pacific Ocean as absolutely solid rock is that it is obviously much too much like an auditorium full of people cheering and stamping feet.

NEW YEAR'S RESOLUTIONS

Yes, I'll admit that I have been sinful. For one full year I had been having a love affair with the number four. That was back in 1974. But we all love best what we know best! All that time, 1975 was practically a mere cipher to me. Then, suddenly, the affair was over. But, oh, the love poems I wrote! Beautiful verses, believe me; flowing verses that wrung the heart. But that's been over for some time now—for nearly six years in fact. True, I remained fundamentally faithful to the one I am wedded to, the number 19. Then again, lately I envisioned an 8, and she really caught my eye. Also a zero: that is, a real child. Somewhat underaged, even. My difficulties obviously get deeper every day. In addition to that, I must confess that the year 2000 always did give me an erection. My pornography is the next century.

January 1, 1980

THE SEARCH FOR THE SOURCE

I can't imagine where it comes from, but surely there must be a source for this all, somewhere. True, streams can be seen sometimes, using a dowsing-rod, or even if you simply look carefully under rocks with a flashlight at midnight; but this source isn't so easy to find. In fact, the harder you look, the more it disappears; and all you can think about is that since it doesn't seem to be prevalent anywhere near the surface, perhaps it's someplace else, perhaps it's down at the center of the earth somewhere—who knows? It's not an easy thing to grasp, perhaps it's better to skip the entire subject. Why am I bothering to write this all down, anyway? Here I am with a poetry almost empty of encouraging imagery. On the other hand, nothing you can do can change what you know. Last week, for example, there was a major critic from Milwaukee who said (making a rich metaphor) that he found my inspiration "a bit dry"; not to mention my wife. *He* meant that the flow was always awful. God knows what *she* meant. I suppose that all I'm supposed to have left is a lot of water pouring all over my face. But maybe that's enough, though; maybe that's all the source there ever was or will be; maybe I've found it now, whether I'm laughing or crying now, maybe I can truthfully say at last that I've never been happier.

from

Universe & Persephone's Telephone

THE TRAGIC LANDSCAPE

The tragic landscape, the only true tragic landscape in which one must believe, the tragic landscape of the medicine cabinet, waits in the bathroom like a battlefield strewn with the fragments of various abandoned hopes. Here, at the far end of the apartment, the very least of our expectations is expressed. The gauze bandage rolls, the thick tape, the mercurochromes and iodines, the blue pills and the pink, the green pills and the yellow, all attest to what we already know: that we will never be free from injury. Moreover, the sleeping pills announce that it is hard to doze, and the No-Doz pills confess to something worse: that it is even harder to stay awake. And as time and the expectation of any relief whatsoever cease, the medicine cabinet fills up still further. This is one of those mornings following a party when one wonders simultaneously whether it is filled up enough to be effective or whether it won't eventually end up by falling off the wall. Staggering around, we remember the stranger at last night's party who smiled in a curious way that seemed somehow to promise a new life—or at least another system than this—perhaps in a place heretofore unforeseen. And as usual, one last time, last night, we smiled back. But today, sinister tissues are whispering of sickly expectations; all too soon, the medicine cabinet may be supplemented by a floor trunk, at best full of various indescribable prosthetic appliances.

PICNICKING IN THE INFINITE

The absolute is fun to visit but I certainly wouldn't want to live there. This way, right on schedule, and more or less like clockwork, we have a pleasant journey roughly every three weeks. Mother brings the umbrellas and her husband, Uncle Fred the sandwiches for the infinite to eat. It's a relatively easy drive from where we are to where we want to be; and the kids of course are singing all the way and so make the trip seem even shorter. Once we get to the site which is the location of the infinite, the kids organize a treasure hunt; they are looking for artifacts native to the region so that we can deduce, finally, where we are. Lots of shouting, more singing, and affectionate teasing while the treasure-hunt goes on. A few of the younger people begin to disappear behind haystacks. Characteristic after characteristic is discovered. We are just beginning to deduce and otherwise and sensibly capture the essential nature of this region and are just beginning to wonder if there isn't perhaps a series of tourist cabins somewhere nearby, when a distant bell begins to chime in a misty building silhouetted somewhere on the horizon. It sounds like a church—but from where we are, instead, it resembles a suite of offices. It probably tastes like baby's jellybeans, sounds like a funeral oration, or smells like blazing fires.... So, longing for home, we all jump back into the car and drive back to the place and time we started out from. We're back before we even know we've left! In fact, already, isn't it as if we'd never left at all?

STRONG TASTES

Strong Tastes: spices in spaces at the rear of kitchen cabinets slowly burning holes in their canisters. Perfumes that hurt. Visions that sprain the eyes, sounds so loud they prevent thought. Occasionally, dangerous acquaintances who carry around models of cliffs off which you will be the first to fall. Fatal secrets confided to Hollywood gossip columnists. Appearing nude on national television; or cockeyed out of one's mind, before The Society for the Preservation of Logic. Trust in quicksand, cats that scratch, and a pet plant with tentacles strong enough to drag one under. Also, a ticket for an American Airlines flight to Arkansas, wearing a beard and long, uncombed hair; strumming a guitar, and determined to tell everyone in the Ku Klux Klan there about your liking for Martin Luther King. Love thine enemies. Despair of power. Long, optimistic dreams about the immediate present; and a new suit of clothing that almost walks off down the street without you. And at the far side of the desert of deprivation and indulgence, or of any kind of extreme or excess, this vast oasis: one strong glass of pure, clear blue water so natural and correct, that it is absolutely impossible to ever recover from it.

POEM TO BE LOOKED AT DURING A NAUSEATING WAR THAT IS MAKING EVERYBODY SICK

If you could see everybody as they sleep, if you could see how likely they are to assume the defenseless and trustful positions that the active body remembers best by relapsing, by imaging silently into flesh; if you could see the closed eyes, the mouth half-open as if expecting to be fed, the hair almost perfectly combed by the repeated multiple purity of random motions; if you could see the arms curved against the sides and the hands half-curled under, fists and wrists loose and good for fighting nothing; if you could see the legs, too, bent not for advancing or receding, but poised as if for leaping straight up; if you could see clearly, surpassing these uselessly dubious professional assertions in all directions; if you could see just once, without the usual slogans, speeches, or any speech at all, without even the possibility of infection from the angering sight of wounds which both sides reveal or conceal for the sake of TV cameras—just once lifting vision beyond journalism, the 6 p.m. news, or Walter Cronkite—if you could see it, even if you didn't see it in color, come to think of it, even if you didn't happen to see everybody, maybe just a few sleepers from the immediate region, East Side or West Side, if you could see it and the wind was right, that is, if conditions were favorable, if you could manage only a glimpse even at this late date, you might still see this world, you might be convinced that the first dreams are still the final dreams, and that these first and final dreams are neither of exploitation nor imperialism.

IN PRAISE OF CHILDREN (I)

Looking around all the time, as we do, on this earth, focusing as we do so clearly on everything that is visible, we sometimes tend to overlook things. For example, the fact that not only is everybody human, but everybody is some kind of child. Yes, the great secret wisdom of Mother Earth, the one thing she verily knows and will tell us about should we care to listen, yet which we continue to react with respect to, as if we might still be ignorant, is that THE ENTIRE HUMAN RACE HAS ALWAYS CONSISTED OF CHILDREN! Different sizes, shapes, and ages, it is true—some unlikely in their manifestations, and so unfortunately isolated in their sad, melancholy, and/or underprivileged predicaments, it's as if they had never been born—But all, all are children. *Everybody* is children! The fact is that the only fully formed adult who will probably ever be located will probably be some secret forgotten amoeba, clinging to the underside of Time, in empty space. That indisputable patriarch will obviously have been there, still, since at least the dawn of creation—so go ahead, oh, my dear, and oh, my also somewhat obdurate children, go ahead and try to send *him* your Father's Day cards.

CORNELIA AND HER FRIENDS

A conversation with Cornelia about her friends. People love to meet them, she says. There's Harry—he's kind of quiet, and stupefied by everything, yet manages to amuse everybody by sitting in a corner and staring at the wall with his thumb in his mouth. There's St. Angelo—he likes to make kites and is covered from head to foot with a kind of fine, yellow down. There's Lemuel Mole—his vocabulary includes a complete repertoire of underground subway sounds. He's also good at imitating the plumbing. There's the one they call The Nameless One—he's up there on the roof right now, a halo around his head, fixing up a pair of wax wings for himself, in honor of his "Enthusiasm for the Infinite." Some company! Then, one night, whispering in a dark place, Cornelia tells you she's throwing a party for all her favorite people; and you're to be her guest of honor.

ARNOLD

I still don't quite know what to make of my best friend, the one on the city hockey team who used to play right wing while I used to play left wing. And we had such a good time, afterwards, in the country where we once set up our booth, and he sold painted clam-shells and I sold lemonade at 5 cents the sip or the shell. But then, somehow, he became a famous lawyer and I became a famous golfer. But—quite apart from that—what I still can't quite make out is what just happened last night. His wife, Sandra, called me up to say that he had just floated off into space like a bubble, and to ask had he, even in his childhood years, ever gone and done that before? "Really?" I commented coldly, "A bubble?" "Yes," she snapped, "a bubble." It was then that I knew she was lying; she was lousy with her lies. The well-known saying is right, about an elephant's memory being like a famous golfer's. *I* knew what he must have resembled, as he floated off into outer space—no bubble; but his back like a beak, his legs like a couple of fuselages, his knees like fleas, and his lips like lovely ailerons. I'm sure that the soles of his feet, in black silhouette as he ascended, were flipping happily around in a dance, like black angel wings. And oh, I'm sure that his outline must have been just like a pretty pink heart. Oh, Arnold, did you have anything to say as you left us all forever? Oh, Arnold, Arnold, you and your stupid name, oh you, my long lost true love, lost long before any golf or the law.

LANDSCAPE

I saw the famous bearded little old man by the side of the road, sitting cross-legged and singing to himself. "What are you doing, famous bearded little old man," I asked. "I'm fishing," he said, "and since you were obviously about to be so inquisitive as to ask me, what I'm fishing for here is your life." "But what are you using as bait?" "I'm fishing for your life using your dreams." "And the water? I don't see any." "There isn't any water," the old gentleman said, giggling to himself, then laughing like hell. "Famous bearded little old man," I cried, "how can you be so satisfied with your purely allegorical life?" The famous little old bearded man gave his famous reply of not answering, and left after folding up the landscape and slipping it under his arm.

PERSEPHONE'S TELEPHONE (I—III)

(1) Persephone's telephone; already, her last message was received a long time ago; and still, all I can see are flowers flying through the air, flowers flying from the mouthpiece, flowers softly falling on my lap and filtering through my ear. Petals are slowly surrounding these black metal centers, making a ring, as in a series of circles at a festival composed of high-waisted yet ageless and somehow young women. Their hair comes as unusually far down as their waists rise unusually high up; and for all the sense they give of having a fine feeling for dress, all they are ever really wearing are single individual petals. (2) When Persephone first telephoned, the ringing was like a string of seeds. Every intermittent silence was like a leaf. In any case, you poured the cornucopia of Persephone's ideas in your ears for many hours. (3) With others, your conversations were more brief. For example, there was another talkative woman who still stops you in the street and threatens you with a revolver if you do not want to speak with her; and simply since she is always blackmailing you, you never want to speak to her. This is the angel with the pistol. By now, you know that when you see her pointing her revolver at you, you can be sure of two things: that she is either threatening the entire earth with some impossible revolution, or else boring you to death by enticing you to invite her out for a midnight drink, and her idea of a good time is tears.

THE CREMATORIUM OF BOREDOM

What's that murmur of voices? All the angels are still over there in the GYMNASIUM OF SELF-CONCERN, hopping around after each other on pogo sticks, trying to get each other to listen to their life stories. The trouble is that the angels know all too well what to expect from other angels; everyone in there knows in advance that no life will be pure enough except his or her own. Also, there is this problem of dullness. Since they spend so much time in this sanctuary, there is almost nothing whatsoever to tell. But despite the seeming unattractiveness of this kind of life, apparently it has its appeal, and such an ideal of sanctity is accessible to even the most general of publics and the commonest of men and women; because now the huge room is so crowded it is almost packed to the ceiling; and the air in there is so full of leaping bodies that nearly all the air has either been displaced or polluted, so that there are now more angels than air, and the angels are now the air, and the air is now the angels. So let the custodian of new customs come; let him change the sign on the door from THE GYMNASIUM OF SELF-CONCERN to THE CREMATORIUM OF BOREDOM; take a match yourself, let it burn down slowly in that narrow, sticky air.

SECRET SINGING

Even in sleep, an undreamt virtue: Secret singing in cracked and ancient pots, mumbling in tunnels and fantasies behind closed doors; quirks in mechanisms, schematic drawings inexplicably casting long shadows; denouements beneath bridges with stealthy hands, sneaky fingers, investigative probes, and incipient pinches; also the explorer who sails by the reef he was sent to find, the captain who dances darkly on the sly with his sail; the unsentimental mental adventurer who dares dream that the brains and bodies of ugly apes are neither golden nor magnificent but rather ape-like; and so here I chant outright to the joy of secrecy, if only I could make myself tear up this paper.

DESIRE AND ITS CONDUITS

Suddenly there are pipes running downward from our desire; who put them there anyway? If the pipes are short and efficient, the engineers must be our friends; is there any quality we love our friends for more than their best wishes for the accomplishment of our best wishes; for their joy in our joy; in short, for their love of our love? But what is this noise we hear now from the other side of the hill? Between you and me, my love, my delight, my interest, or my constant concern, an enormous waterworks has recently been constructed. The waterworks is a system of pipes so enormous, so complicated, and so cluttered that it can only be compared with the system to be found beneath the kitchen sinks in households of any elaborateness whatsoever, or in bachelor apartments located in buildings with inept plumbers. And even as I write these words, I can hear a certain amount of clanking beginning and voices calling for further elaborations. It seems as if already the water is running more slowly, new pipes are being inserted in the system every minute. And the civil engineers are not only explaining these complications by saying that the old wells have given out, but by saying that now there are others who need water as well. Which only goes to show even more than Marx or Marcuse or Mickey Mouse how the economy of scarcity is always assaulting the economy of excess and ecstasy. My love, my delight, my interest, or my constant concern, fear this jealousy of thirsty joy; prepare for the shock when, some day, stepping into bed, you slip your foot into a system of tubing as elaborate as that of Boulder Dam. Later on, to take our place, as well as that of all other lovers, this particular government will no doubt recommend sending in a staff of trained civil servants fully authorized to hold each other's hands, get "serious" with each other, gossip about others, steal a kiss, and go courting, in what they consider "earnest."

ACCOMPLICES

(1) At St. Polyana's party, everybody is so bored that all they can find to talk about is whether or not other people might be enjoying themselves elsewhere. Also, whether or not some other guest who happens to be there, and whom you have met for the very first time, is actually your long-lost or secret lover. So let it be your best bliss to tell them yes; and for the most anxious guests, let both of you describe your most intimate and-as-yet non-existent activities in vivid detail. (2) Then, at some later and larger party, after you have actually begun keeping company, enter the room at long intervals and through separate doorways, and pretend that not only is your former love over, but that you have actually begun to positively hate each other. Start these envious people thinking that when you gave them the information they wanted and needed to hear in the first place, that maybe *then* you were holding something back from them, and maybe *then* you were lying. (3) And as a special treat for professional gossips, drive them into frenzies by standing in opposite corners of the room with veiled twinkles in your eyes, insisting in curiously inflected tones of voice that you don't really know each other very well, just "only barely." (4) Walk together invisibly hand in hand; see to it that your passage in any direction is simply a generous extension of the bed—where, as everybody knows, nothing is ever accomplished with pleasure except for those things in which you are absolute accomplices. (5) The Bed: a place where you will finally perform like two undercover agents. Get into bed with hats pulled down low over your eyes and dressed only in shiny shoulder-holsters. And when you get out of bed again, let your best behavior be that of two gunmen, aiming the truth of your feelings at this world and its curious inhabitants.

from

The Badminton At Great Barrington; Or, Gustave Mahler & The Chattanooga Choo-Choo

&

"Puffton Poems (Poems from Amherst)"

SATURDAY NIGHT AND SUNDAY NIGHT BLUES

That kiss was a mess. It kept ducking
As if it had just remembered a worm underwater
It had missed a moment ago, it slipped
From her beak

But we're going to Zora Crawshaw's party on Sunday.

Nor was the hug much. It was more like a tackle
Who has intercepted a forward pass, and has had to avoid
A wrathful oncoming quarterback in the end zone.
I ended clutching an article of furniture
Pretending it was necessary to lean.

Still, we're going to Zora Crawshaw's party on Sunday.

As for getting to bed, she kept referring
To a springless mattress on the floor two rooms away
With curious interest. I meant the big brass one. To clarify
Her position, she threw a pillow
Into the bathtub, several sheets, herself, and her nightgown.

But she has invited me to Zora Crawshaw's party on Sunday.

Are we really as close as all this domestic intimacy suggests
To her? Are we really ready for that lifetime of laughter
She promised in the past? Is *King Lear* a comedy,
And *Medea* mere comic relief? I shall dwell on this
For a while; and dwell alone, without her and her daughter and her laughter.

But when I went to Zora Crawshaw's party on Sunday
She introduced me as her lover.

I TRIED

I tried to reach you in poems, I tried to reach
You by semaphore, I also tried to reach you through toots
Upon a little toy trumpet, but all to no avail.
Except the time I tried to reach you with a pair
Of golden calipers, and bit off your toe flaming red.
Also, I knew I had gotten through to your favorite pet wombat
Once, that time I offered it a dollar bill
Not to look when we necked at a movie matinee.
I have met other souls, plunged up to the hips
In mist, most times, and stabbed them in the stomach
At the weenie-roast, but never with such results.
This is a case of confusing *I love you* with *where*
Are you, and the room number on the hotel key won't tell.

PORTLAND TAXIS

If I were on Mars, and wanted to get back-to-home, I would
Hail a taxi. There's nothing I like better
Than hailing a taxi; they have saved me many times
From the spectre of fiscal responsibility. From the bottom
Of a well comes my voice, hailing a taxi, Get me
Out of this oubliette! Beside the bed where I make love
The business cards of taxi companies are tacked up.
Taxicab salesmen surround my every motion
Hinting I'd be better off as a driver, but it's
Hailing a taxi I relish, not threading my way
All day through the midtown traffic. Busses won't do
Either—the exquisite squalidness and rash of
Public transportation is not the point—but
Something about these little moving cubicles
Filled with me on demand. I feel crammed-in on a plane
Because there is no room for me to lift my arm, there,
To hail a cab. In a cab there's no room to hail
A cab, but then you are already in one; it's ridiculous
To even think of, unless you have the hots
For hailing a cab, thousands of cabs, as I do. But then I
Digress; I wish a taxi would come, grind and screech
To a halt, and take me someplace, anyplace else, and get me out of this,
Such as, to Portland.

WHERE

Where, oh where, are the love lyrics
Written by people with excellent vocabularies,
Where are the songs that exercise the throat
Of the mind?—Without this embarrassing racket
About what you're supposed to be feeling
And at what time, as if emotion were a clock radio.
I'm tired of coming on as if I just fell off.
You, we're people of intelligence, aren't we,
And can tell a labyrinth from a cherry-stone,
Can't we, anytime we want?
                                        The loudspeaker boomed:
"Dr. Laurel wanted for surgery; another partner
Is getting flakey in the recreation room. Dr.
Nobel-Prize, a crazed humanist is running amuck
A few feet from your collection of antique sideboards."
What could I do? I patterned myself

To resemble the wallpaper and the cutlery
In the cafeteria, and now I will have to pay the consequences
With a $3 bill, with your portrait on it,
My love, just like everybody else.

REUNION: THE FOURTH OF JULY

Surprise! Fourth of July!—those fireworks in these pants
Match those in the sky; she's back, and it's almost sexy
The way we fused (that one last reunion), the light from a "Chinese
    Tumbling-Person"
Drifting across her cheek, fading out.
Nobody predicted it would be easy, with two
Psychological firecrackers like us; our friends stood back
And waited for the fall-out to fall. And those were our friends!
Our enemies were practically beside themselves

When I took her little hand in mine, and bit it
To a pulp. Or when she kicked a hole in my TV set
When I wasn't looking at her. Dire prognostications
Were delivered from Delphi; it was inevitable
That Something Happen. It has. Hardly anybody's dead yet
From this. It has a way of just quietly going on being
Absolutely hysterical. *Sweetie, turn your weary peepers*

To the "Cornucopia of Ambiguous Comestibles," now falling
At our feet. Tonight, even our rotten nation
Has a constitutional right to celebrate.

THE AGREEABLE WEEKEND

"'It's not important to me, it's not
Important to me,' I hear myself repeating.
Then I lie down and slobber on the floor for a year.
That's repression, isn't it, Doctor?" "Yes,"
He says, "don't forget to kvetch
At every available opportunity, occasionally
Stopping to burn down a house or throw a tantrum."
And me, with my old ideas about "discipline,"
My controlled use of the present tense
So as to make it appear that I wasn't here.
Now, the concept of "here" grows obsessively present.
When you bother me, I don't want you around.

I'm not even nostalgic to replay our Greatest Hits
In bed. I refuse to cross that doormat
To our former future which you are always dragging out
Of your prognostication closet. I don't believe it, and I don't
Remember it. All I know is that when you're here
It's either better or worse than if you weren't.
Worse, last time, it wasn't. And I want to tell you that
Before I forget, because to me that's what's important.

STYLES OF ORGASM

In Memory, Wilhelm Reich

There's the one that goes "beep beep"
And comes barreling down the highway,
Tells you when to come, following after
Like Jack falling down and breaking his crown—
About Jill I'll spare you the further details. Then
There's the one that never seems to happen—
The neck gets stiff, the body's a Nazi,
The eyes go goo-goo, spinning around
Like twin targets, pinwheels fizzing, so slow
It's almost perpetual—you can always bet that that person's
One who seldom sweeps her house. She needs money
Or a servant, she says, or her long-lost Pop. Then there's
Shades in between, shades of gray, or better yet,
Rainbows, their shadows on the windows—I know all them—
Can light up a room's interior, but there's too many
To recount here—and then I'm not trained
In analyzing all but the obvious; even that's
Only an extrapolation of intense experience. I'm not
A social service agency, am I, just a *schlep-*
Along poet, and already I'm released
By this poem: in this case you can hear my laughter
Affectionate as a Mafia prisoner's daughter
On visiting day; she's brought along a cake
With the well-known file in it, the alarm-bell's
Ringing like wedding bells, and all that
The warden knows, scratching his head, at this point
Is that once again, God knows how, some goofball's got off.

THE DIARY

Daylight: Clean up cat-shit, write a poem, clean up some more
Cat-shit, read a poem, hang around the house, don't think of poetry,
Don't think of anything, as usual. Hang up the telephone. Fiercely! Bang!
Though no one is going to call
Either in or out of here.
The fortress is rumored to be impenetrable. The archers are ready already
        anyway,
And back there they are boiling up the oil.
At the desk, we sit like a moat.
Later in the day, tea. The Ladies Auxiliary would like to auction the fortress
Off, with you in it. The Salvation Army would like to. Alicia would like to.
        Very interesting
Mothers, but *noli me tangere*; & still later, meditation on dental work.

A little vodka with buffalo grass in the glass
Will get you through the poetry reading in the evening, in fact will get you
To give one. The podium in the bathroom
Is beneath the bathroom mirror where you mutter & mumble.
A look in the bedroom mirror to see if your head is still on
& So to bed! Papa Bear & Mama Bear move over to make room
For you. There is an axe between them. The bedcurtains are drawn on their
        sweet dreams.

Moonlight flickers over the towers
And mad perspectives of the interior
And its curious inhabitant.

UP THE HILL

So. Here we go. Up the street and up the stairs
And up the hill of Golgotha, as you told her
When she answered the buzzer. "Golgotha?"
Mandy said, and then looked blank. Long discussion
Follows, the usual stuff, mostly about trust
And how I'd begun to lack it, in Mandy, in me.
Exhausting. Some refreshments, then, which I took;
Then Mandy asks if I'd like to take a look
At her roofgarden! Out the window and up the little ladder
To the tarpaper. You shake. It's partly because of the vodka
And partly because of her, and partly because of the phobia
Of heights you've had since you were three years old
And Uncle Joe took you on the parachute ride
At the World's Fair and said he'd push you off.
But not Mandy. All Mandy wanted to do (again I quote her)
Was supply "an intermission to the discussion."
So you climbed the last step to Golgotha,
To be greeted by spryer Mandy, who showed the way
To a place where two old friends could comfortably lay
Surrounded by fifty cross-shaped TV antennae.

LETTER TO JIM / MAY, 1975

Four weeks ago you racked up in the Chevy; last
Night I went up drunk
To fix the TV antenna, yet; stumbled, and of course
Fell in a lucky direction, got these skinned knees
Only, to prove it, plus also I'm writing this
So I must have survived.
                                        Tate, I think
Something's amiss. It's obvious
We've been killing ourselves, and there is still a future in that
But if anybody thinks I'm going to recommend it
Here, they can forget it. I, for one, think we're certainly charming, don't you,
So why this near double-wreck?
An unhappy life, some boring business about the car
or the TV, nope. It's not being grieved, I believe,
That is making the days a mess
But "Never Enough Pleasure," that's my motto.
                                                                        So where do you draw the line?
—Sometimes I feel like a fool in school without a ruler,
Not knowing when to stop until I drop, then
Maybe I just begin to get a message, but not much. It's still not too clear,
Quite. But a little. It's not that we lack sufficient fear
Of death; fear of Dearth
Is more like it; a desire not to be missing
Anywhere. Problem is, if we don't take care
We're going to end up short a limb or a life.
                                                                And there I must admit my fear, dear
Jim; it's that one day I'm going to wake up and find
I'm short one Tate; that is, I may wake up and drop in to the general
Lunchcounter of delight and call for a Tate to go with it, and hear
"Sorry, connoisseur, there just ain't no James left today."
And believe me, Jim, that would do it; it would end the appetite
—Not the taste for Tate—but
The one for life, very nicely. It would not kill a philosophy,

But how could there not be guilt? Old pal at the bacchanal,
Old partner in the ridiculous, there would be guilt; first
On my part, because I would never have told you what I think
I think we're doing, tonight having figured it out a bit. Sometimes
I think we get it wrong.
Sometimes I think
In our cups we are too full of complaint.
Because what's painful is that we would both be so joyful—
I wonder if it's possible. I have no doubt
We'll be the first to find out
But to do that, we'll have to be around for a while. So, smile,
We have more research to do, the rest to dissect,
And I never saw a corpse at a microscope. So, let's stop
For a minute and consider this: We're both going
For broke, but the only hope of getting there is to miss.

So can we agree? Will you promise
To take it easy on that obscure midnight blacktop
If I promise not to wander around at midnight, feeling alone on some god-
forsaken rooftop?

—Michael

FROM POEMS AROUND THE HOME

What tiny things enormous emotions cling to. Amorphous
Thoughts, how you clasp on and fasten to the most modest
Items around the home, around the world. Like a rock
Hostessing a hundred thousand barnacles
What unwanted weight visits upon you. Innocent, patient
Toaster, afflicted medicine-cabinet, poor, put-upon napkinholder,
Telephone and toothbrush (sad victims of human demand:
"Love me more! Love me more! Love me more!").
I understand why you must escape.

[. . .]

[THERE IS SO MUCH IN LIFE THAT POETRY]

There is so much in life that poetry
Is afraid to touch. Where are the longed-for lyric poems
About money? My favorite Latin-American poet
Is a Puerto-Rican who lives in New York
And complains about the cockroaches
With gusto. With almost no gusto, I listen
To lyric poems about your soul, about your aunt who wanted
To be a great painter, but raised 58 nephews
And one niece instead, leaving you with a
Crappy responsibility and a sore piano.
Here, in the land of languishing anguishes
I plunk down my little time bomb. Here, from
Beneath my balloon, in a gondola loaded with tombstones
On a distant hill, I wait for reports.

BYE-BYE TO SOMEBODY

I want to write something crazed and pained
In a new way. What is the stomachache of the heart
I am at pains to know, but probably not sufficiently
Badly. It's characteristic
Of Eskimos to do funny things
With dogs, and I understand there is one tribe of Indians
Who prize not the baby, but how much the birth hurts.
They decorate the mother with dental floss
And lead her into their version of the subway, where she is allowed
To jump the turnstile, while the band plays
"The March of the Dwarves," or something else appropriate
For framing. I want to return to that nation
Of clapping bicuspids, where nobody is out to kill
Or maim with a verb, or break your neck with a carefully placed
Semi-colon, where the sweetness alone
Could execute a felon. Parenthetical dropsy? Unheard
Of. That's the place! There, when we part company
On a bridge and depart toward opposite ends,
We arrive alive, and smiling, approaching. Let's
Share a disaster, anything
But this. Anything but this violent bitching
And spit. This determination with respect to
Finality. This enthusiasm for truncation in the face
Of the possibility of lingering on. Agh, I have suffered from a lack of respect
    for tentativeness
For the last time. Max, pass me the salt
So I may anoint a teardrop. Fiscal responsibility
Is coming my way, the sensitivity of the bombed-out
Thrush on my window-ledge, before I slam the sash—
All kinds of good things, between spleen
And conscious indifference. Where am I? Where was I? How could
You do this to me, on the evening of
The hockey tournament; my high-diving act

Is suffering terribly, over there in the corner.
You have left me alone with my book and that old tutu
Of yours, stuffed with a former tissue paper, retained as a reminder
Is the best I can do. It will self-destruct, you say,
In such-and-such a number of minutes. Tradition
Is not your strong point. "The pleasures of a day-to-day existence
On a hand-to-mouth basis . . ."—Can't I trust anybody
Anymore? If you would only betray everything entirely already
And in an entirely original way, then this poetry would pay
Me to write. But all these half-way measures
In the interest of definitiveness? This way, there is a hole. This way,
There is an absent center. This way, the Gods
I invoke are over across the street somewhere,
Nursing a beer and ogling the Wurlitzer.
This way, lots of things, but none of them that great
Tragic sense that might, finally, hand us all a laugh.

from

Family Blessings / Family Curses

FROM LIKE MANY OTHER NECESSARILY PERIPATETIC AMERICANS, AN AMERICAN WRITER "MOVES HOUSE" FROM ONE CITY TO ANOTHER IN ORDER TO TAKE UP A NEW JOB—RELOCATING FOR REASONS OF FINANCIAL NEED, LEAVING HIS NATIVE NEW YORK CITY (WHERE HE'S LIVED ALL HIS LIFE) FOR BOSTON (A CITY WHERE HE'S NOT LIVED BEFORE); HOWEVER, SINCE ACCEPTANCE OF JOB OFFER INVITING HIM TO BE "VISITING PROF. OF ENGLISH & C.W." AT BOSTON UNIVERSITY HAS, MONTHS BEFORE, ALREADY CONTRIBUTED MUCH TO THE FINAL BREAK-UP OF AN ALREADY SHAKY MARRIAGE, HE TRAVELS WITH DIVORCE-PROCEEDINGS ALSO UNDER WAY TOWARDS SEVERAL NEW & UNFAMILIAR DESTINATIONS, SOMEWHAT DISORIENTEDLY, & WITH ONLY HIS CAT FOR COMPANY (SEPT. 1, 1977)

Here's where I find myself currently:
I'm afloat mid-flight, poised (sorta) around noontime, in a window-facing seat, & crowded in with lots of the usual-seeming computer-type commercial travelers, in one of the good old "Eastern Airlines" busily shuttling jetplanes
On a so-called "Routine Run" (Flight # 353) from New York City—where I've lived all of my life—& bound now for the city of Boston
—A city located in what pilots call, U.S.A.'s "East Coast Corridor," north of N.Y.C. only about 200 miles more (but which might as well be located on the moon as far as I'm concerned, since—though I've heard that Boston is a pleasant little city—it's a place I've never lived in before)
Yet where, starting today in fact, by agreed-upon formal & informal understandings ("Gentleman's Agreements," & then a one-year plus-

maybe-more academic contract), it seems I'll be living for at least one year (& maybe two full years; &—who knows?—"Just Possibly" even three);

& 'Tho, by glancing around (probably somewhat nervously), I can clearly see that whereas most of the passengers also on board here are looking sorta bored, i.e., traveling quite commuter-cucumber cool & casual,

Some few even semi-snoozing, & most merely lightly chit-chatting, laughing, rattling their newspapers & talking (mainly) about the weather

I'm not doing that; & so that tells me, too, how much I'm diff'rent

From those others here, packed in so calmly & so serene—together like vegetables in a salad, or lotsa proverbial sardines;

—& The casual way they're all looking & acting aside, my own mind, too, is working overtime to remind me (& that's the way it really gets most to me!)

That what's happening with me here & now

Isn't what most reasonable people in their right minds would ever call "Routine"; no, no, I think, but rather is

The key event in what often is—for most of us stability-loving adult earthlings—a far more serious, unsettling, & sometimes even quite disorienting process:

I.e., & Ay me! (plus also, oy vey), here is me—a relative homebody— & today, yes, this very day, I'm "Moving House."

—& Moving, fact is, not just towards one or two fresh destinies—i.e., to a new city for me (which happens to be Boston)—& where (as it also happens), waiting for me are four big blank walls (between which I've never been before);

But actually towards several types of "Major Changes," which I'm bound now to explore—

To wit, & to phrase it short (feeling odd as all get out, I made out this list in anguish—& as if to reassure myself that I'd reason to feel so nutso—whilst pacing the floor & smoking up a storm, back in the "Departure Lounge," back at LaGuardia airport):

Big Change #1:—Besides moving away from my dear old immense, various, & well-known as the somewot crazily lunatic-energetic American "Literary Capital" city of N.Y.C.

I'm on the way to landing today for a rather foreseeably long stay (*Big Change #2*), in Boston, well-known as an American "Academic Capital"—(but which is well-known also as a smaller & a lot more conservative city)

So as to start, (*Big Change #3*) a new job, e.g., as "Visiting Professor of English & Creative Writing" at Boston University—Ah!, an august title to be sure

With (starting in September) very many tempting & very welcome dollars to match (poets, like lotsa other people, being known for living in a kinda perpetual financial crunch); but also t'was B.U. which required of its temporary "Visiting Professor"-to-be there

That he grab everything from his pens & pencils, the 20,000 reference-books in his own home's library, goods, chattels, bric-&-brac, stamp-collection, stuffed owls, plus pots & pans & furniture

To set up a whole new household practically from scratch. (I must admit, it interests me to see if the distractions oft attendant to practicalities of such resettlement can really do much to help one bear down & teach!)

—Anyway, the ink had hardly dried on signed formal "Academic-Contract Agreement" lines, when (some months before) suddenly along came *Big Change #4* (I list it as "#4" 'cause indeed I started living with it some months before—already, it's a fact that's a large part of this traveler's slowly disappearing past, & not of the immediate future):

Which was, that just after contractual negotiations had finally reached completion, my wife of some 15 years (spouse dreading, as she said, "Trials & Tribulations" of new-city re-location) decided that moving to a new city (even or especially only for a relatively short while) wasn't too much to her liking

& Thus, & so, nerves did fray, & give way; & tempers did finally explode, & so, like a swallow that migrates at the start of spring, she fled nest of her own accord (which next thing I knew, two lawyers were referring to as her "Former Manhattan Abode")

Alas, she shedding ire all along the way; & with, in her wake, me, too, among her diverse divestments
Hinting (tho' a feather could then have knocked me over, 'cause I really felt quite innocent of it), at my so-called plans for nefarious "Abandonment."

Ah well, ah well, enuf of that, enuf of that—for what I can say today to speak plain
Is that—feeling quite abandoned & sad & somewot lost myself; (&, I must confess, just a li'l bit angry)—
Rather like the landing of this airplane, divorces can't come summarily enuf; & soon enuf for me.

—& So, for at least four big reasons (plus a too-numerous-to-mention collection of oddly-assorted little ones)
Like this cloudy sky thickening suddenly before all of us travelers today—& accumulating heavy cumulus in potentially soggy masses against the blue,
Blowing the first of its stormy graynesses already now against right-hand wingtip, wing, & shrouding o'er at least two of our four shining jet-engines, too
—& Thus, & so, like the whole general goddamn atmosphere up here,
Now suddenly become unclear (first, sev'ral random flashes flying; coalescing, secondly, into noisy bolts & points of crazily zig-zagging light'ning),
I'm feeling, as are some others here (who now I see themselves aren't chatting & laughing so much anymore—& who've already begun cross-examining the Stewardess for bits of "In-Flight Info.," instead of extracting their big news from the newspapers)
Just a li'l bit "Up In The Air."

—& So, yes, I guess that well-known "Fear of the Unknown" hath right now generally got its hold on me
& So I'm not, now I realize, like most others here, paying so much attention to all that terrible & ever-so-threatening thunder & light'ning

—In fact, I must admit, midst my overall vista of long-range meditations, I
rather think of them as charming, delightful, & picturesque (if
relatively irrelevant & distraction) interruptions
Although—I must confess also—like other people I do sometimes stay
awake some nights
Tossing & turning; & having my share of nightmares about things like being
drop't from heights & falling...
Still, I try not to be all that much of a "'Fraidy-cat" about heights.

—Anyway, even as my now also agitated fellow passengers (many actually
chomping fingernails) are worrying & wondering duly
About little matters like whether we're going to fall down out of the sky
(sev'ral of them evidently suff'ring "Anxiety-panic Attacks," & enquiring
with straight faces of a greatly amused stewardess as to whether this
here airplane will now serve "Complimentary Drinks"—with some even
demanding in a flurry of raised voices as to whether there are such
things as refunds on used Eastern airline shuttle-flight tickets)
I roll, & I roll my eyes to the skies midst the sound of their complaints
& So, discover over Southern New England somewhere (for that's about
where we are now, I figure),
That somehow, still, I can remember how to smile

—Perhaps partly also because, just beyond the water-shedding right-hand-
wingtip (which is the one I'm so fortunate as to be looking at)
I just now spotted one good strong ray of sunlight;

*

& So, as if to celebrate with my dear Alice, the airplane journey's end
(Eastern's "routine" Sept. 1, '77, Flight #353, hath both took off &
landed, actually)
I reach through one of the cat-carrier's five tiny vent-holes with one of my
spare little fingers (where I can still just see Alice's pink nose showing)
& Tickle tickle the little whiskers of my tiny little friend;
& I can understand, that she may be more nervous than even me, & still
more full of fears

—For after all, as it is not—even with many "homebodies"—& as it is with many kitties,
It's her first time out-of-doors in approximately 10 years.

*

& Then, together with all those others, I'm standing there on the Departure Gate line;
&, This time (except for maybe some nervousness expressed by my looking in again & again at Alice), I know my state of mind's OK
At least, compared to that of my fellow somewhat visibly shook-up & upset travelers
—Many of whom I'm kind of sorry to see ('tho I guess it's also sorta funny) are now sporting white barf bag-tops like white flags flapping from the pockets of their suit-jackets &/or their raincoats
—Tho' it's true I realize I'm now performing some rather frenzied physical juggling, shifting my three items of hand-luggage from right side to left side of my arms to circulate the weight
For purposes of immediate comfort, now that we've all landed here in Boston:
The academic briefcase, the cat-carrier of course—plus the one loosely & obviously hastily-string-wrapped & apparently perfectly empty carton.

[...]

FOR GERALD FENICHEL (WHO, "WAY BACK" IN 1947, LIVED "WAY BACK" IN N.Y.C.)

Sometimes, during periods of rapid change in our lives, we find ourselves searching for meaning in the deep past: & remembering, & reflecting on, roots.

—Psychology Today *(1977)*

Suddenly, like a cloud of Wheaties
Taking the shape of a boxing-glove, or a pickle
That appears in a salad in the midst
Of some perfectly ordinary & even uninteresting
Lettuce-leaves, returneth Gerald Fenichel.

I'll tell you about aforesaid Fenichel
Because otherwise it wouldn't be serious
Using his historically hoary and dignified
Name like that; he was a distant relative
Of Otto Fenichel, the famous psychologist. At this point

I should also tell you two other things: Gerald
Was a friend of mine from adolescence
(We were in both public school & the boy-scouts
Together; I'll go back to the details later);
& I just looked up Otto in Erick Berne's famous

Layman's Guide to Psychiatry & Psycho-
Analysis, & he was indexed on page 157,
Except that there's nothing about him on p. 157,
Mr. Berne's book is positively full of typos
So I can't tell you anything about this Otto

Or understand my friendship with Gerald
Via that background, so I'll have to tell you
(I'd really best do so; & so I'm sorry, Otto)
Directly: Gerald & I were so-called "Friendly Enemies"
So full of enmity we used to be blindfolded

& Beat each other over the head with boxing-gloves
For the amusement of the scout-troop during meetings;
& Then there was the terrible spectacle
Of our wrestling each other every day after school;
After which, we'd go to his house, & sit around

& Watch what was to become the early history
Of television, i.e., "Kukla, Fran & Ollie";
& On Tuesday nights, there was Milton Berle.
You can't get that kind of hot stuff from Berne
Had his book been indexed properly, even;

& You can't get the flavor of my love for Gerald—
& I think his for me—so that when we were fighting
Each other, it was like making love, all that touching
Under the guise of masculine competition, all that looking
At television, which was also more like fighting

Because it was then, looking at that little screen, that I felt so distant, so lost,
so cut off. . . ;
Oh yes, come to think of it, you can get
That flavor or feeling, just look for example at my old love poems about
women
They, or me, approaching then avoiding, touching & then withdrawing;
Perhaps, in some sense, that's all I've ever written about,

—You, Gerald, probably a fat doctor or maybe some kind of head-shrinker,
Because I think that was what you thought you were destined to be,
Not (as some kids used to call it) a fat "Faggot," which is also not what I've
turned out to be
Either; I don't know exactly what I am now: "Mercifully Celibate"
At the moment it would indeed seem to be;—but from where I am now

To wherever you may be, "Hail & Farewell," Fenichel;
—Next time I'm in New York I'll look you up in the phonebook
Or consult the A.M.A. for your name; & so maybe even if you're not there
You somehow will be & so we'll meet for a beer, & argue over
One or two points, perhaps; & it will be like old times.

[Boston, Nov., 1977]

FROM TO PEGGY GABSON, ALREADY BACK IN HER NATIVE N.C., FROM ME, ALREADY BACK IN MY NATIVE N.Y.C., IN ANTICIPATION OF FURTHER MEETINGS IN BOSTON

"Hi!," Peggy!, & less abstractly, & less casually—& so's to keep in touch with int'resting you at once, following our recent chance meeting, initial conversations, & mutual introductions
& Also, so as to confound this second act of oft-goofy-fate, which finds us already so many miles away from where we met; & already (I think), too soon separate
May I—hoping to continue to spare us both the usual conventional guessing-games & secrecy—
Tell you a few things more about me:

For years, if I can remember, I used to act a whole lot like reality was a kind of optical illusion, projected
By me, in my spare time, sort of. (Well, I guess that's how lotsa people acted
If, at one time, they hadda mostly "Innerly-Inclined Mind"—& so was "Just a 'Dreamy Kid'.")
&, Although I guess like almost everybody, I'd rather not ever have changed my mind, & started acting any diff'rently,
Things feel different, lately, all right, to me. How? I dunno if I can say how, 'zactly—but somehow now
It all sorta feels like the diff'rence
Between a purple cow, & the puce pom-poms
On a cheerleader's costume (the skirt part)
—That is, one thinks one grasps what "It" is; & yet one doesn't.
Well, there are mysteries in life, doesn't that explain it?
So, I guess what philosophers say is right, hooray!;—reality's a mix of personal internals, with certain externals (& also a few other things) added in.

Now, when I think that some phenomena's "Out There," & that it exists in its own right, sorta unprojected (& 'specially if self-contained li'l me might go so far as to want to reach out to it)

I like if I can or may, right away
To find out a whole lot more about it—or, as they say, to "Check It Out."
Well, I guess maybe every serious adult—if they're not too rushed by events
  or confused by events & in a state of general upset—likes to do a li'l
  bit of that—

Peggy, you told me too, for example, also that when you
Were a kid, way back when; instead of accepting the life you were born to
  back in N.C. there, lock, stock & barrel, & hook, line & sinker, etc.—
You found, early on, that you too hadda kinda "Innerly-inclined" critique to
  make: & so, as you too grew, learned also to look over lotsa things
  carefully so as to "Check Them Out";
& Thus, lively Peggy was soon considered there (as indeed lively Peggy
  might be considered anywhere) to be a so-called "Difficult Individual";
  & even some kind of wild & terrible "Rebel";
—Well, I approve; Peggy, & think that's just the price that some people have
  to pay, for being
Just a little bit daring, & original.

[…]

DON HALL & JANE KENYON OF "EAGLES POND FARM," IN NEW HAMPSHIRE, INVITE A N.Y.C. BOY, RESETTLED FOR A TIME IN BOSTON, TO A COUNTRY PARTY; &, FOLLOWING AN APPROPRIATE IF BRIEF "RE-ORIENTATION SESSION," EVERYBODY GOES OUT TO HEAR SOME POETRY AT "THE BLAZING STAR GRANGE" IN DANBURY, N.H., AT KATE FOWLER'S 100TH (!) BIRTHDAY PARTY, JULY 16, 1978

One of the primary problems for the composer in an industrial society like that of America is to achieve integration to find justification for the life of art in the life about him.

—Aaron Copland

It wasn't my land, it was your land, up they-ah. So, for me, it was a bit like theatre
(At first), not only to have Boston there as point of departure, but also to find myself still farther away—way up North here—in the middle of New Hampshire.
Twice-a-tourist, at Ms. Kate Fowler's 100th (!) Birthday Party. It was held

(Stranger still), in one of the "Grange"-places "The Blazing Star" that they had
Built, farmer-folk, almost a full century ago, so as to hold meetings against various Eastern-urban railroad barons
Who wanted to go running express-trains through their cow-pastures & their barns

Or who (worse yet!) envisioned railroadyards & coalyards where there grew grainfields. Doubtless, I thought, Old Kate,
Don't forget, what that was like (perhaps even as she made her entrance there—all faces turned towards her from afar—that sunlight-bright

Door, so many yards off in "The Star"; Yes, turned toward Kate, suddenly present among us at last here, calm in shining new wheelchair, in pretty white party-dress, her smiling, tiny, pretty face beaming keenly from above its nice clear collar; then looking thoughtful withal, as Kate moved forth toward her audience beside one staunch grange wall—)

&, As Kate went by us, gesturing to & greeting nearby "Grange" neighbors bending down as if quasi-curtseying, to whisper things to her, in passing as it were. I

Scann'd (in the background), various common dec'rative plaques along the grange-walls, some of them (as Don had said), with various names of the Halls'

Relatives engraved thereupon;—& yea, in the midst of that plaque-plethora, beside me, Don, & Jane pointed out some more.

&, Looking & waiting, located temporarily here midst all this well-situated history, this trav'ler had to remind himself, somewhat as if for stability:

So, here it is, somewhere forward of the last quarter of the Twentieth Century

&, Here I was, in this midst of it, sitting firmly there as could be; &, finally, slowly arrived up front before all her folks, there was a very old patient lady, quietly awaiting her centennial ceremony;

—Oh, calm pois'd Kate, evincing at odd moments some slight fidget-disconcertment, but fundamentally seeming not at all surprised to have turned up here today, situated there in her fabulously shiny & perhaps for all I knew new chrome-model tubular-structure wheelchair;

& There was that sudden applause & also a surprise-message being recited slowly now by the flowery-flannel'd snappy-shirted M.C.-of-the-affair:

A personal homespun message (via telegram) from her U.S. president, Carter

& Wife Rosalind; & this living, personal moment in a region's history was thrilling everybody & (even stranger still), twice-a-stranger here, me; & yet rightly, it seemed, somehow quite rightly;

& Suddenly beside me & beside themselves those dear sweeties Don & Jane
was largely weeping in the seats (they had sat down on either side
Of me; & this was trav'ler-kindly, & made me feel kind of like family);

& There was Jane shedding some lovely large globs & there was Don most
tenderly misting
(For this was happening almost exactly on the literal land that they live on,
as those plaques I could not help but keep accord, kept reminding-me-insisting);
& Next thing we all knew there was a suddenly azzif-from-nowhere young
lady singer down on one knee crouching beside Kate then uttering
also her own tender All beside that wheelchair

Almost as if before some present-day secular U.S. of A. altar, the young lady
singer now bent over herself—but still steadying Kate Fowler's tired
hand with gestures of her own hand & exchanging gaze-for-gaze &
adding her own memento to the day with her own birthday-keeping,
& time & history-honoring song-message—
Singing what was described as a "Kate Old Favorite," nothing less than "God
Be With You, 'Till We Meet Again"—a tune from by-gone days yet full
of positive sentiment appropriate at that moment-spot, the main
point there & then being the presentness of the past, & the serious
importance to all of us serious humans present here, of the sense of
dearly remembering
(—& I still can think with aw'd astonishment at the effect of her brave art:
that young lady singer actually compressing her own diaphragm with
her own one free hand; she so clearly & absolutely determin'd to
secure one hard-to-reach still-distant virtuosic superb high-note which
she wanted to—& indeed, did—actually at last make);
& That made sense, too, at that particular historic site & date, for to
celebrate right then & there with what wd. most please Kate, her art,
was after all that musician's whole point;
—& Just then, as if in accompaniment to that generously-given, tenderly
tendered, movingly-memorializing song-message
What was announced as "The Official Birthday-Celebration Poem" was read
aloud

—Composed, I heard from Don, by a literarily-inclined relative of Don, &
of Jane; & I suppose it was what the relative-poet himself & some of
us all would call
"Occasional," all set up so immediate touching-neat in its direct & feeling
couplets;
& I could not help but be moved by it, the poetry from start-to-finish
expressing nothing but the best of external circumstantial sentiments
on this historical day;

& So moved was everybody else, in the rows all around us; to the very edges
of that grange, I saw numerous verges & surges of tears & many other
visible tiny evidences of interior (those latter evinced by delicate meek
twitches of meek public restraint); & there was something else in
there
Besides that, that spoke out freely for me: I liked the definite fact
That tho' writ most assuredly for a sweet-nostalgic party, that work wasn't
frilly, or superfluous, in the sense that it was accomplishing something

As, in Kate Fowler's birth-century, poets—self-bespoke "Unacknowledged
Legislators" of all the world so many long & accumulat'd songs ago
Once said poetry should do (&, I think, once again ought to try to do)—;&
anyway, certainly, from the depths of its directness
That poem made an old lady & I think somehow all of us who were there

Feel a whole lot definitely better—Evoking, & perhaps making us more
aware, of surviving American heritage, & perhaps, the richness of our
own age—(& Don himself said in a quiet aside, that later
He'd have to be sure to pay his compliments to the cousin who was its
author);
—& Some children, then, tabled a few yards away behind a great cake

Where they had been row-sat in manageable pocket as if for security & who
were poised now murmuringly somewhere on the edge
Of youthful rambunctiousness semi-sized-in-places & on some metal chairs,
As if signal'd secretly, came all forward & deposit'd some small token
presents & mementos & flowerlets in Kate's hands, & upon her lap;—
wotta great flood

Of gen'ral joy & relief there was then, the very good thing to do, having been done; & followed thereafter
An outflux of folks saying "Greetings" & "How Are You" & "Where've You Been"
An influx of gen'ral cake-nibblings & there were various sociable millings & smilings just inside those suddenly thrown-open late daylight-showing great old meeting-house doors (there was a guest-book on a tiny table there I asked Jane & Don during one spare clear moment "Should I?—May I Sign It?"—they said, "Sure!")!

—& Then we left trudging out into a sudden rush of late (tho' still-bright) afternoon summer crossing up one sloping-up side-street of the hilly little town of Danbury, to their car
(Me with a bus-timetable riding now like a rock in one of my jacket-pockets);
& We drove, wending by what major side-roads there were there, using well what remain'd of returning-time leisure,

Towards many immense stone hills that lay along the way back-at Eagle Pond Farm; oh, hills in which lay
Many Hall relatives, many Kenestons, Fentons, Wells, & Halls,—& all Don's (& now also, all Jane's people:
Amaz'd, aw'd, I heard of hillside upon hillside with their bones; like grain-rows, they were suddenly everywhere I could see hills & fields with ranks of lined-up gravestones; even the bones were staunchly situated & well-settled among those peacefully landscaped-girt, countryside U.S. farms & homes

Themselves securely enfortressed, behind stone walls, property after property; & then after some further timely pointing-outs & honoring observations, that, too, was done, Don & Jane imparting yet another time-honoring continuity-evoking true memorial vision;

&, As, sunken deep in thoughtful-quiet, all those three trav'lers drove on, I let my mind go wand'ring . . . —& it went straight back again, to the grange; &, in particular to a small mural

I'd seen on one large wall there, behind which Old Kate (then the subject of
most of the looking-at), sat;
Picturing a simple old homestead, in its to-me-strange serenity & solidity, it
reminded me now suddenly
Of the Hall's own historic home at Eagle Pond Farm—a staunch old white
house, country-modest, yet substantial, because so compact & neat—
& all in all to my mind, certainly a comfort:
So "Earthly," almost maternal there; & somehow (e'en to me) so natural &
relaxing in its presence there, settled in surroundings of its calm-
inducing pond; with also, there (in the distance, far above & yet a part
of it all) (tho' towering up there in the air & all in all far above it all)
The fierce shelt'ring fortitude of still more solidly grand (tho' locally
nicknamed "Ragged") Mountain;

& I tho't then, again, of all ('neath that towering protection given somehow
by Kearsage Mountain) that the Halls' car was happily coming back
to;
—& I envisioned again; & again re-me-be-tho't (this vision was flashback'd
one-part; & one part flash-forward'd)
Particularly, oh yes (for some reason), most very particularly

Of the good old stock of well-worn family tools & artifacts equipment
I'd espied in the Hall family attic (where, the night before, as he introduced
me a bit to Hall family history, Don had showed it to me),
Which became now suddenly & strangely like a general background to all
the NH scenes that I had (today) more recently seen:
—Oh, tho' wrapped securely in that attic beneath unsuccessfully
dissembling sheets of ancient or recent picturesque dust, oh, *there*
were up there (as I'd earlier seen):
Big pins & shears, oh old butterchurns & hammers & parts of one old
broke-up but still treadl'd sewing machine; oh boxes with neatly
carded but still wholly unspun wool, plus numerous half-opened-up
plus loaded-up trunks;
All to my dazzl'd astonished eyes indeed most thond'rously presents; & oh,
beside sev'ral complete full tool-boxes laid open with contents only
faintly rust-bristling, there were there, too, many fine & curious old
playthings

—Looming highchairs diversely & fantastically curliqued; & dolls; & doll
furniture; & spare dolls' eyes & extra doll limbs & some noses
Peeping out from 'neath numberless & numberless pretty-parti-colored
paper boxes—heaped up beside masses of old sleds & only faintly
time-tarnished tiny kid's & also some adult-sized skies—;
& Oh, there were scatter'd about, sepia postcards photo-albums (with room
for them, & still ample space for yet others to come around them), in
serried solidity there, all stacked up; & carpet-bags; plus pursed & still
further
Clutchpurses, open'd to lovely rich cloth linings, & beaded o'er & flower'd;
& then there were too, the old family coverlets, which seem'd
somehow twice secure, the coverlets themselves covered o'er with
their weblets;

—& Lamps, there were, lamps shaded & unshaded, all (as I saw them)
colored-rosy (e'en tho' currently unaglow)...; plus clocks; whole
families of clocks; grand-
Father & grandmother & grand-daughter & grand-niece & nephew, & yes
Clocks with all kinds of still more relatively fantastic kindred connection &
interconnections by way of spare & maybe still interchangeable clock-
parts, such as
Hands, oh there were many multiple bundles of spare clock-hands piled
behind some clock-faces gone unsprung, their various dozen hourly
numbers in diverse type-styles flung out in all directions as if
attempting to count up everything that had happened & that was
maybe perhaps some day to come (that attic's accumulated richness
of history alone, almost exceeding all evocation—not to mention
literal description);... & then (at a road-bump

I mentally snapped back to the somewhat similarly dusty windswept rising
country road we were on then
Flanked on either side
By a few old wood (but mostly red-brick; & many new cement) schoolhouses
where (at that moment in history & time-spot) children were not—
vacation-time then being relaxed U.S. decree
For celebrating a very dear & (but for whispers almost silent) nice old lady's
100th birthday-party

& For a vacation, too, from learning about "The Space Age & Modern Technology" & who can tell what other futuristically sophisticated things—such as "How The Language of Our Art Must Be Much Different From Our Own"—that is, from the one we daily needs must use
In getting our daily things done; poetic language *supposedly* being (as in the past, too, in schools it was once taught)

Less readily handy & solidly earthy than "Exquisite" & "Implicit" & "Symbolic"; & somehow less material, too
Than that which people choose for their literal & actual daily use; so then again
For the third (& final) time that quiet late-afternoon driving-time my own mind struggled burst free &/ or carried on
To the Trav'ler's Legacy that was awaiting me courtesy of Greyhound, Gray Line, Trailways, or Vermont Transit; to the unused green ticket in my inner jacket pocket that would take me to my "Home":
To Boston, where I'd just relatively recently moved

& To the brief thank-you note midst scanning bills already stack'd up, I knew I would wish soon to write in mem'ry of that visit, on the one piece of equipment,
Working or other, I have now left from my own deep past; oh, there on my own batter'd old writing desk, there where it would it would my father's old Smith-Corona Galaxie II
Typewriter which he got late in life to learn his fresh skill of typing on while dying, dying slowly, years ago, of his cancer, that
Typewriter, that typewriter which is not quite an artifact yet; that green travel-ticket & my blue, sky-blue working typewriter . . .

& So (still during that quiet driving-time) my mind, too, came to calm; & it continued, that calm, all the way into Don & Jane's pebbl'd driveway there beside the homestead lawn
Buildings, of Eagle Pond Farm—Eagle Pond Farm, where suddenly we drove up all together & arriv'd all at once

& To bound out & wave to each other all oddly as if somehow all we three
travelers had all come a great distance
To once again get to greet each other upon that lovely, large calm green
lawn; & yet once again, inside ('twixt quick glancings at my bus-
schedule as hastily I caught up my pre-pack'd overnight kit) (& as Jane
& Don bustled about in yet another room getting some evening things
in better order for later), it milled around some more, did my mind

(As indeed it can still mill) around, all around, the non-cement concept of
how—during those few strong strange precious moments we are given
(& which are doubtless yet due in our lives), it feels—truly & somehow
lastingly & solidly—feels to us
Those rare times when schools are out, & there is at last at least some tiny,
calm interim time
For attending, finally, to the steady, continuous music
Accompanying & (sometimes) even happily blessing
All of our living earthly things.

[Boston, 1978—N.Y.C., 1987]

XMAS ON BAY STATE ROAD, BOSTON, BY B.U., 1978

In fond Memory, Alice Hoop

It's Xmas almost Xmas & hardly anybody home
Around here, here in Boston, where I've been living; at least t'seems they've
    all gone off—
Every student & (seems stranger yet) every local Prof.—
Oh, so fleeting, & how oft, the joys of "Intellectual 'Communities'"!—
All, all gone off to their serious, "Serious Life."
—Seldom have I seen so many weighty, truly serious suitcases
In the hands of so many virtually total strangers.

& Me, today, I go poking moseyingly around my campus-edge
Apartment's red-brick, thru streets strip't now of their usual local color;
Bright winter clothing gone, hardly even a double-parked "Boston U." —
    stickered car here
Give relief to this background of almost total, concrete gray;
Oh, it's been one year & ½, almost exactly, since B.U. invited me (from
    N.Y.C.)
To be their peripatetic "Visiting Prof.," in both Engl. & C.W. Depts., for
    poetry;
—'Cept they said, "move up here, too"—which whimsical invitation it
    turned out meant (as such oft doth for "Colorfully-living," that is,
    cash-short vagabond poet
It was for me & me alone to locate & search out

Like an instant local real-estate expert, my one-room convenient-to-B.U.
    apartment to negotiate, furnish, & rent
In the midst (no less) of a still ongoing, tho' dragging-on, N.Y.C. marital
    divorcement. True,
I had company, for a while, in a little 16-year-old white cat
"Alice," she was subject of several ongoing poems, who '78 saw surface
    cancerous. Following major operation
She died, at start of term-time, as leaves fell, in the fall. But if I was,

In the midst of this, tense from matters rather demandingly domestic,
forensic, esthetic, plus financial & therefore whil'st dealing with all these, somewhat
Bizzy-crazy nobody, least of all most folks at host B.U., cared to

Ask the poet why. & so, as host to these sad thoughts on Xmas Eve I wander
Suddenly I espy it: a recently & much-too-early tossed-out (for still fresh) little Xmas tree
Behind a store, green fir tip sticking up invitingly from out a dumpster,
All untinselled o'er as yet; & withal a paper-scrap memo-pad sign taped to it
Requesting, "PLEASE TAKE ME" Sweet!—its identity evidently, too, this later
'78 day, come 'round as Xmas throwaway. & So I lifts this tree
Joyfully from out the surrounding trash (thanking the Good Lord that
If there had been bugs on it, I wd not have flinched, thinking "Oh Horrors" anymore, or even batted
A single eyelash); but not, it's quite clear, clean, almost pristinely; & so I can think, almost immediately,
To wit: does I have any decorations to go with it? Oh yes, oh thank the Holy Spirit
Of Personkind, & of Human Ingeniousness, oh, yes, I guess; I see deep-down
I must still be undiscouraged; for roughly 10 days ago, returning pre-holiday-time
From an early closing bookstore, I recalls I bought some Xmas balls
At 5¢ & 10¢-store o'er in sparkling town of Cambridge;

Matter-of-fact (the deep mem'ry says I'm suddenly flooded by)
I also bought myself a set of little flickering lights (at dime-store), perhaps for Xmas meant
Or else my close-of-divorcement-conclusion year to celebrate, which midst haste
At term-end, I just set all still-in-box at the edge of my couch
Near one big bay window, & left on, winking & flashing. . . ; Oh, but why?—

I suppose only to show anybody still left sentient in this transient district
walking by
That I'd survived; was still alive; & still wished a Merry Xmas

To them; & also hoping, I suppose, secretly, that somebody'd see it
(Surviving, too, it seems, is my sense of the fantastic) & invite me
Mayhap, to Xmas party-visit. But now I got an Xmas tree oh yes an Xmas
tree
Which I fleet-foot off like some itinerant academic Tiny Tim across Bay
State Road with,
Evergreen over shoulder, & with hardly a needle falling; & back home in my
room
I find an old plant-pot left from summertime, so's to set it up,
Using some old root-drainage rocks as chocks (I checks

To see that they're dry, 'case lately my wearied system, I think
Has had enough shocks). & in its pot, at the center of my brown carpet
It stands upright! A regular traditional Xmas landscape! & So then I run
Briefly, backtrackwards, with enthusiasm, as far as corner grocer, the ever-
open
"24 Hour Village Food Store" (where I'm relatively well-known persona
gratia
For my former insomnia), all so just to supplement, at least at last minute,
my
Bits-&-pieces hall-decking supply; & for my

One large bare room with its two big bay windows now winter-dim I buy
A plastic envelope containing 20 multicolored ribbon-bows;
—& Also, out of keen-focusing side-eye, spies I

(On counter-corner), six smashed-up candy-canes, just remnants,
Which I decide to run home the one brief block without; but then, I think
Having multicolored tree galore, with the ribbons,
& With the Xmas-balls from my half-forgot hall closet be-decking store
(& After shaking the tree, to recheck out the chocks,

My dear fir-tree, from which still no evergreen needle doth unsightly fall),
"Why
Some of them candy-canes still had the hook-on part intact!";
& So I run back after counting out 60 pennies
(All spare change that had been accumulating lately)
& Leaning o'er the counter I announce to the store-manager:
"It's a true Xmas-in-Boston Neighborhood Miracle, here's a customer

Thinking of buying three of those still-priced-at 20¢ candy-canes; any bargains?
—But he don't blink a grizzled eyelash, I heard once that famous book-banning Boston
Could oft also be a hostile, self-contained city ("Townie" local-folk
Oft forbidding here to apparent-transient "Gownies"); but this reaction's not only
Proper-Bostonian, tight-lipped-humorless but ridiculous!—& so, smiling, rushes I out
Parting with all pence & hangs I the three half-intact candy-canes from the lower-limbs
Of the tree; then plugs I in the (now) unboxed-at-leisure light-bulb-string in & on

& Oh What Glory O Wot Glory (& OhmiGod this reads almost
Like a regular early-earthly Xmas-story!); then sits I down
& Turns around on my couch & begins to admire it
As, amazingly, cheerily, it glows its pure improvised light against the street;
& Then, some yesterday fresh-bought pure cow egg-nog in my hand
I relaxes, & flips on the b&w household portable T.V.—
('77 saw vanish the color-one, by property-settling decree—)

& Watches I the Pope & several reverend-folk offering talks
& Enlightening holiday-time meditations to dinner-tabl'd Christians;
Yet, in the midst of happily beholding milling throngs happily I wonder a bit too
(I hope not too oddly, but rather out of natural human curiosity): just who

It was, not long ago, left behind that brand new Xmas tree?
—Some affluent student, who tho't he or she wd spend pre-Xmas
In Boston locally, but who then panicked & optioned-out "Home-sickly"?;
some well-loved, family-

Supported sport, who gen'rusly offered the tree's odors for a few hours
To room-mates; & as for imminent prodigal home-flight return, completely
planned it?
Oh, times have been I felt like the most woebegone creature on this planet
—'Cept all this whole fucking tree's beautiful now, in its glow
On a little table beside my bedstead with its worn-out leftover-from-
marriage coverlet
Where, towards the midnight, I saw fit all at once transplanted it
(For reasons half-unknown to me, not sure I understand it)

—All I know is I felt almost glowing & peaceful too, suddenly, as I lie down
beneath it;
& Somehow feel that tho' it's already nearing midnight
It might be nice, since this tree's so pretty, if I shared it;
& Since once again at year-end I'm thinking of my dear at-sweet-sixteen
dead & cremated cat
I haul across the apartment a small wicker basket I kept (it must be
confessed), with her modest little ceramic ashes-urn in it; & thus lying
down
Beneath the tree & beside this literal & real souvenir
Of my old companion (with a single chaste candle burning bright beside it)
I spent with Alice early, unaccustomed dawning hours, discoursing
philosophically
On various events since her deceasement. &, compared to the larger part of
1977 & 1978, those
For me, most curious-strenuous of years, this hour is so peaceful-calm as
slowly it registers. & perhaps, too,
Suitably, at noonday, lights still flickering in their chain, Alice
Snug in her porcelain casket, inside the wicker-work basket, the candle out
(As I suppose is only appropriate), I awake to find me beneath the tree

—& Xmas Day's so decent, so calm, & so fine (being at last my own; & my
own's own, pain-free, & with present self's & with almost all other
memory absent)—that I find I can even
Resist (especially upon this occasion) making analogies arcane, specious, &
old-time literary;
For example, I shall not even compare my Xmas tree
With the enormous shared tree in Rockefeller Center in N.Y.C.
Midst another lost host of gone but never I swear never-to-be-forgotten
company;
Various old fast friends, the dozens, who, midst times that were hard,
banded together as one, to help send me this year's Xmas card.

from

Transitions

&

Of:

ELEGY FOR EDDIE (MY STEPFATHER, BRIEFLY)

For my Mother, Helen Davis Benedikt Sachs,
(b. 1911–d. 1988), who re-married in 1978;
& In Memory of Edward Sachs (b. 1909–d. 1979)

1.

He was, I suppose, what many people would consider a perfectly ordinary, &
even quite conventional, man; but—whether or not that was true—
For me, of course, he meant something special.

& Naturally, since he was my new stepfather, I wanted to get to know him a
whole lot better,
This stranger to us both, who had entered my mother's life—despite the
differences in our backgrounds & interests, & the so-called
"Generation Gap," etc.;

—& Yet, as my mother had once warned me, he once told her openly, that
he did not understand the purpose of my, or any other person,
writing poetry;
& So, I supposed, at the time, *that* was the main reason why meeting with
him finally, would not be easy,
& Why it might be difficult for me to relate to him; & for him to relate to me.

2.

—Alas, for me, that generally genial, elderly, yet somehow still peculiarly
youthful; totally grey-haired, yet still entirely lion-maned, strong &
handsome man,

Who, at the start of the summer I was being divorced (no less!),
Began dwelling with my mother, in my mother's, & my decade-ago-deceased
father's, little vacation summerhouse at Point Lookout, on Long
Island's south shore

Where I, too, had once spent summers; &, as the saying goes, "Grown Up."

3.

& So, at a meeting which my mother had (after some resistance from me!)
finally, & laboriously, set up—for late one summer afternoon, around
cocktail-time—
We found ourselves there in that rather warm, sunny, summer living-room,
before a big, cut-glass pitcher of iced-tea, with multitudinous hors
d'oeuvres plates scattered around everywhere,

Among furniture I remembered from my childhood:

—Down to the big gray wingchair Eddie was sitting on, the polished maple
rocker my mother was sitting on, & the little, beat-up green vinyl
hassock with the purple plastic mat on it
Which I'd settled down on, once again, for that particular afternoon.

4.

—& Though mutual pleasantries were exchanged generally, with my mother
looking on nervously; & smiling somehow rather girlishly; & trying
(really quite heroically, it occurs to me only now in retrospect), to be
equally attentive to us both,
Filling & then re-filling our glasses of iced tea insistently, as if she feared
(perhaps wisely) that there might have been some danger
In hauling out the cocktail supplies, with the potential volatilities that might
attend to vodka;
& As if she recognized too, that quite apart from the weather, both her new
husband, & her only son as well, might have been thirsty, especially,
on the particular, hot mid-summer day

Nonetheless, a kind of deeper chilliness prevailed, colder than the ice-cubes,
even; & scarier, somehow, than even the burning weather
—Perhaps natural, too, I guess, in view of the difficulties that time
entailed…

5.

& So, despite the affection shown by my dear mom to her new husband, &
me both

Replete with alternating hugs from her to him & from her to me, & then also
to us both—&, of course, vice-versa (which latter, I can remember
plainly, rather embarrassed her, since she ducked away as if avoiding
them);
& With Eddie doing almost all the talking, reminiscing about his business,
pre-retirement, to the doubtless somewhat grimacing individual,
whom he referred to, repeatedly, only as "Helen's Son, The Poet"
(He'd once been, much to my probably barely-concealed chagrin, a
salesman at, & then an owner of, a used-car lot)

The afternoon wore on slowly, limping uncomfortably towards what seemed
designed by my dear mom to be, its rather curious & (as it turned
out), rather curiously anti-climactic, grand finale:

6.
Which came in the later afternoon, towards sunset, almost at twilight,

When all at once, & much to my surprise, Eddie himself requested that I
read him a couple of poems chosen by my mother, from my books of
published poetry;
—But more or less half-heartedly, as if deep down he thought it really
unnecessary;
Perhaps since, as he said, my mother had already, time-&-again, proudly as
a mother hen
Shown him, I guess by way of introduction, some books of mine she kept on
hand, in the tiny library at the summerhouse
—Half-heartedly, yes, I sensed; but then my mother absolutely insisted on
it, as we approached that day's oncoming sunset.

7.
Still, pleased, more or less, of course; & wanting my mom to hear something
that I'd written relatively recently
I read to them both, instead, from a copy of a literary magazine I'd brought
to give to my doting mom—a couple of then brand-new poems about
(of all things!), my mediocre marriage & even far worse divorce.
—& Though that was probably not exactly brilliant of me (among
newlyweds certainly), anyway, it seemed somehow to fill the bill . . .

8.

—& Though my mother thanked me afterwards, taking the opportunity
again then, as a dutiful hostess sometimes will, to scurry to her coffee-table,
To pour out for us all (yes!) yet another round of rousingly ice-cold tea

Her husband did not think to thank me for that effort, afterwards;
But rather (& rather like a jerk, was what I could not help but think then),
quipped, & wisecracked generally, about poetry;
—&, Especially, about what he called its "Absolute Impracticality"

—As if nothing at all unusual had just happened, before him, in that living-room, then; & certainly nothing to modify, much less, soften, his prior opinion.
(Still, I held my tongue—holding it down, I can still recall well, as if with
1000 pounds of, say, crashing-down, rhinoceros-shaped paperweights!)

9.

Oddly enough, I still cherish a Polaroid snapshot taken of us three that day;

—It was taken by a neighbor, via flash-camera, both by Eddie's & by my
mom's request, during the closing moments of that somewhat strained & stressful, yet uneventful day,
When all our trials (except for saying our goodbyes), were all over;

—It's slightly faded now, somewhat beat-up & dog-eared; & already, with
some of its emulsion worn off & gone
As happens, sometimes, with even the very best of photographs
& Though it doesn't really capture the full flavor of the day, as for example a
poem can (or, at least, can try to),
Still, as I've said, I still cherish it; & even keep it kind of handy, in a file copy
of the magazine from which I read from those two once brand-new poems, that day—it's useful still for sure, at least as a sort of bookmark;

—& So, there once again, is Eddie, whom, alas—one year after that meeting
that mid-summer so long ago; & so soon also after the beginning of
his & my mom's marriage,
Suffered (ironically, while working on something on his car) a sudden, &
fatal, heart attack;
—Looking, of course, in the photograph, still generally genial; & somehow
peculiarly youthful; & of course still lion-maned; & still quite strong &
handsome—&, of course, still smiling!;
—& There, of course, is also me, looking, too, of course, as I did then
(smiling, yet bemused somewhat, I suppose that one might say);

—& There, once again, is my mother—who died only some few years
later—looking of course as she did then, too:

With my mom posed at the very center of the picture, still looking
amazingly poised; yet still smiling shyly, in her strangely girlish way;
& Yet smiling somehow proudly, too, like a bird about to sing, or maybe like
the proverbial cat who has just caught the proverbial canary; & with a
twinkle in her eye (unless of course, that is purely due to some
reflection caused by camera-angle);
& With Eddie & me standing there on either side of her, each with one,
opposing arm, around her waist; & with broad grins, too; or just
possibly both even laughing outright, it looks like, from those broad
grins—perhaps, for all I know, like my mom, out of some sense of
deep relief also;

—& Though Eddie was, then, like my mother, also about age 70
You would practically have to look at the beat-up, fading, somewhat
inadequate Polaroid with a magnifying-glass

To detect even a single wrinkle between them.

THE FOURTH OF JULY & NEW YORK & NEW JERSEY & LAURA & ME

New Jersey, along the western Hudson shore, where my sweet lady Laura doth dwell, in handsome high-rise facing Upper West Side Manhattan, hath big cliffs (they're called "The Palisades")
But compared for example to New York City, only relatively small firework-displays on July Fourth.
On the other hand, in Manhattan, along the eastern Hudson shore, where I doth dwell, we get really immense fireworks, but have only relatively tiny cliffs, which are known informally as "The Stone Declivities," which drop down via various zig-zagging stone stairways from Riverside Drive to Riverside Park.

& Since, one Fourth of July nite, I was not smart enuf to accept my darling lady's invitation
To scoot over to her picture-window'd apartment on opposite Hudson shore
To behold in panorama the grand & glorious whiz-bangs (co-sponsored by Macy's) projected o'er Manhattan's skyline
(& Also since the angle-of-vision from my particular digs might not be optimal)

Down those "Stone Declivities" by various stone stairways we did run, carrying a still half-full champagne-bottle, which was certainly picturesque of us, on the night of the "Anniversary of Our Country's Birthday"
& Which was perhaps even inventive of us, especially since those champagne fizzies, midst our bizzy & p'raps overly hardworking lives, happened to be left over
From an as-yet-unsampled-present, given to me around a month before by my dear Laura, for my 55th birthday . . . Anyway

What a great view we got of The Palisades; plus heard we many distant popguns going off, accompanied by faintly flashing lights somewhere on the Jersey side;

& As we stood there holding hands, or sat there smooching on various semi-collapsed Riverside Park benches
Sipping champagne now & then from our long-stemmed glasses, misty company of miscellaneous raucous zealots setting off their own chosen kinds of cherry bombs, & treetop rockets, around us.
In two senses we got, almost, "Bombed."

New York City's & Macy's display we heard but distantly, but almost invisibly over the East River. Best display we could see that year, gazing across the starlit, sparkling Hudson waters (discounting various fleeting flashing from Kennedy, & Newark airplanes above their Hudson River route; & smaller airplanes seeking aerial entertainment; plus nautical pleasurecraft jockeying also in virtually futile & semi-unseemly frenzy, for further views of the occasion, reportedly to be seen along the Hudson)
Were twirlings on the far-off Jersey horizon—which Laura did identify, as emerging bravely "from a tiny little semi-private mini-park, in North Bergen..."

Thinking the occasion over, I remember thinking—as the two of us rambled back upstairs early still carrying champagne glasses & souvenir bottle of that champagne's remains—
& Scooted back towards my apartment with its tiny balconies & shiny, great big French bay windows (duly Windexed by my own hand just the day before)
That we might have looked, to the scattered groups of noisily carefree merrymakers, still assembled relatively riotously down there in Riverside Park—
Yes, with just the two of us there, & departing, alone together—
Like two people in the wrong place at the wrong time.

As we were running away, I wonder, did we look that way? All I can report, is that some passing stranger we passed
(As together we ran swiftly by; & all the way back upstairs, via all those stone stairways)

Did single us out to wish us—as if personally—a "Happy Fourth of July!"—
as if
We two, too, had something serious to do with our USA's Happy
Birthday—& with a certain originality,

On "Independence Day."

FOLONARI RED WINE

1.
There's one thing at least, I think I can count on in life, which is that:
In this, our ever-changing, uncertain, & highly wayward world
My talented 20-year-old next-door rock-performer neighbor in NYC whose lovely, often poignantly yearning but sometimes wildly soaring voice I cannot help but hear as she rehearses
Echoing across our mutual hallway, every weekday morning from Monday thru Friday—

& Who to make ends meet, tells me she has to hold down two jobs—

One job (which she hates), working Mondays thru Fridays as a waitress at a downtown Manhattan cocktail-lounge at suppertime;
& The other job (which she loves), performing on weekends at rock-clubs in the Village as lead singer in a rock-&-roll band—
Will, every Friday night, at the end of her week's waitressing work, regularly set out beside the door of her apartment for recycling
A large white empty carton marked with great big red white & blue letters, spelling out always "Folonari"

—That is, a full case weekly of a dozen empty bottles
Containing lately, lots of red, red wine . . .

2.
& Each Friday night when I see one of those cartons—as I cannot help but do when taking out things to our mutual hallway to recycle, too—
What I find myself imagining first thing, is that for reasons I think I can understand
My next-door neighbor has been celebrating.

Celebrating first of all, finishing up yet another all-too-tedious waitressing week at what she terms her "Regular, Straight-world-gig"—a job

which she insists (like so many other young artists who perform such secondary work to make a living) is "Only a Temporary, Back-up-type Job"
—Temporary since, as she told me once in passing, in a voice wrenched with bitterness & pain, she can't yet find full-time work as a musician;
& Celebrating second of all, the immediate prospect of finally getting away (hooray!) from the things in her regular weekday routine which bore her, in order to perform the more fulfilling work on weekends

Which according to my ears at least, she sounds born for.

3.

& what I also imagine from some of the songs I've heard my talented young neighbor sing, which echo through our mutual hallway & thru my doorway weekday mornings,
With lyrics declaring that "Rock-&-Roll Will Live Forever" & that rock can "Change the World" & maybe even "Revolutionize" it
Is that young as she is, my gifted neighbor already realizes full well
That some of the things which can happen to talented people in this world

Are unfair & sometimes seem almost intolerable.

4.

I realize of course that my description of my young neighbor's lifestyle, replete with speculations on her mostly unspoken hopes & dreams & aspirations
May involve all kinds of fantasy on my part, replete with lots of guesswork & wild & rash assumptions; & that I may be saying all this at the risk of crediting my young neighbor perhaps just a bit too much
By presenting her here—what with her apparent disappointment in "The Real" & her apparent yearning for "The Ideal"—as some kind of profound Greek or Roman thinker
Or maybe American-style, rough-hewn Transcendentalist philosopher

—Someone who goes into action sort of like a soldier, making raids on the boring status quo to earn an uninspiring if modestly sustaining living, week-nights Mondays thru Fridays

Between temporary cease-fires when she performs her music & practices her
art & when the world seems relatively right to her
—On weekends, at her rock-&-roll club-dates, nightly on Saturday & Sunday

—Yes, I realize full well that some of my ideas about my talented, struggling
young neighbor's life in NYC & its related Folonari-carton mystery
May just be pure fantasy on my part & maybe even just plain baloney
& That what's really going on across that hallway is that my talented young
neighbor just may (albeit perhaps somewhat inordinately)

Simply like the taste of "Folonari"

5.

Anyway, whether or not I'm projecting, speaking for myself
I must confess that sometimes I feel the same way about life—an artist's life
especially—that I think my neighbor does
& Sometimes wish on virtually any terms & however temporarily
That I too could find some easy escape or egress or exit by some side-
corridor from the injustices & the tedium & the indifference & the
sheer disorder
Which dominate this world as it now stands
—Especially when it calls for people of talent to perform work to make a
living or
Simply to survive, which they're not best suited for . . .

& Though I myself dislike the taste of alcohol, including wine as well, I try
to take the long view & avoid being judgmental
About what comforts in life may sometimes be taken by worthy people held
back by financial necessity or mere circumstance
—But talented young artists especially,
Who, remembering my own struggling young years, my heart especially
goes out to,

& I suppose that—if taken in moderation—that relatively inexpensive, mild
red wine called "Folonari" is among those things which offer
About as harmless & handy
A temporary vacation from this harsh world as any.

OF FRIENDSHIP VS. CONFLICT-OF-INTEREST: MEDITATIONS FROM AN OFFICE DESK

Friends, friends, what are friends? There are, I sometimes think, some
people who have only what you & I would probably think of as being
only the most minimal definition of the word "Friends"

—By that, it would seem, such people only rather circumscribably mean, at
best,
Simply other people they might find, somehow, to cushion & protect them,
hopefully, from having to live out their working lives, on a day-to-day
basis
Surrounded by an atmosphere of total disdain, abject contempt, & general
hostility
—Thus preventing them from having to endure too many hostile frowns
during their long day's labors; thus invoking also their rather dismal (I
think) version of an "up-beat" or "cheery" atmosphere
Around them, seemingly—but yet not quite exactly—like what you or I
might normally, & rather more celebratively, call
"Bubbles inside of, or afloat above, a champagne-glass"

—In their melancholy case, "Friends" being really only just grim buffers
designed to do the cushioning & blocking, against various maybe even
far worse calamities & catastrophes than censorious frowns
Re their clumsiness, &/or incompetence, from coming disastrously to pass

—So, in *that* case, being surrounded by "Friends" like *that*,
Is, I think, sad; & a bit like someone resigning himself or herself to living
out what is, timewise, certainly a rather significant portion of a life
Walking around at work sheepishly, & with the shuffles; & in the midst of
sheer paranoia
Amidst hordes of possibly only imaginarily self-sworn "Enemies," i.e.,
anyone who may have realized, somewhere along the line what a
slipshod flop their fellow office-worker is,

Protected by fundamentally only half-hearted teams of "Allies," i.e., by their co-workers' own unofficially—or even officially—hired gunmen.

*

Of course, for far too many individuals who think about friends *that* way, the likeliest "Sworn Enemy"
Is probably *reality*. In that case, there's a problem, then, should such a person's so-called "Best Friends Forever"
Be called upon, basically, merely to produce a distraction, so as to dissuade what might otherwise be a healthily reality-facing, independently problem-solving person
From permitting himself or herself at any given point from receiving the obviously very seriously sad impression
That he or she is in fact an ineffectual jerk at doing his or her own work; & that he or she may perhaps be ineffectual in general, at handling anything at all, particularly successfully & well;
& Is thus, perhaps, what we might call a total "Fuck-Up."

—& So, in this way, we come to confront the phenomenon here at our own overly-busy office-desk, piled high with the work we've completed in the "Outgoing" message-box (most of it subverted completely by plethoras of memoranda in the "Incoming" message-box)
Of people who have absolute authority over us, business-wise;
But who are just no good (or even just plain lousy), at their jobs.
—For isn't the abovementioned, all-too-commonplace, & really quite dreary definition of "Friendship," the one, inevitably, we find called into play, for example
By the glad-handing vice-president of some company in re the president of that same company, should it ever be even-so-slightly pointed out
That the incompetent v.p. screw'd up by sloppy mayhap, on the proverbial "Crucial Contract Affecting Everything";
& The definition invoked also by any messy under-foreman of a factory, in re the foreman-in-charge (just in case some simply reasonably grumbling groundling even dares to *hint* that he feels critical, about how the aforementioned messy under-foreman has been running things);

& Then, too, there's the inefficient & uncareful assistant principal of some grammar-school
In re his apparently sincerely but in any case rather suddenly-expressed "Fondness" for the principal-in-chief, who hired her or him—especially should some poor supply-less instructor point out, for example, that the aforementioned assistant principal forgot to sign requisition forms for, for example, all the school-supplies for the forthcoming next one thousand school years (Oh, wotta dangerous-to-students-&-to-education itself goofball individual!; &, Oh wotta danger to all personkind that type of person is, too, not to mention perilous to the mental health of the youth of all the earth!); & yes, sometimes too

Even a poet will sometimes mis-employ the word "Friend" like some grungy misnomer, & wave that word about back & forth in the breeze, in relation to an editor or a critic whom he or she has glad-handed up to the sky above the trees,
So as to impress, or otherwise keep in check, one or another of his or her supposed political "Enemies,"
—Even though that editor or critic, might have really liked, & approved of his or her literary work, quite objectively. In any case, I think that all that's
Bad business; bad sense; & bad Talmud; & is dangerous & besides that stinks, that kind of definition of "Friend;" & all such definitions of "Friendship" are, made merely so as to ward off criticisms of incompetence, or made out of dread-or-fear.
—Ofttimes one can tell quite easily that the term's being misused & abused, because all too often when such a person, usually white-collar'd,
Is caught red-handed, amidst some thoughtless oversight, or lazy malpractice, or worse yet some piece of disgracefully dishonest wrong-doing; & when he or she is directly confronted about it

The classic type of nincompoop to whom I refer here

Will evoke as more or less pukey defense a powerful "Friendship" in still higher, "Higher Places"; & another sure sign of culpability, is that he or she will allude to same, with a certain

Pleased-as-punch-grin we can usually readily recognize & thus can herby
properly classify as "Shit-eating";—like the grin I received only
yesterday for example, accompanying a would-be highly confidential
inter-office verbal memo at "The Angel-Wing Machine-Shop" where I
myself happen to work,
Saying, shamelessly, & in effect:

"Regrets!: All the directives I gave out or otherwise issued forth to our staff,
including you, almost two months ago
& On the basis of which I notice you've been working both your head off &
your heart out since, virtually every night & day,
Were ass-backwards & ill-thought-out; & besides that quite incomplete; &
showed (I must confess to you, in complete confidentiality—especially
since, believe me, even if I put this all in writing, about 15 seconds
later the little piece of memo-paper would be denied by me as coming
from me—& about 20 seconds thereafter, would self-destruct on your
desk like a spy novel)
All the practical & administrative foresight of a 2000-year old brain-
damaged, dyslexic maiden aunt;
But incidentally Dr. Dreadnought the head of this here art establishment
Is a friend of mine & what's more his wife, the highly sociable gentle
Mistress Beelzebub, & mine, the highly sociable Fair Lady Styx,
Spend every single Saturday afternoon at the opera
While his eight kids & mine, who spend every other minute-of-the-week
exchanging baseball cards down at the roller-rink just behind my dear
friend the Mafia concert-master's hideout,
Are the most confirmedly unified aficionados during Sundays
Of various widely-misunderstood sports such as dry-land kayaking,
subterranean lawn-tennis, tongue hockey, & synagogue bingo."

*

—Now, the ages of mankind & the annals of all humankind

Are, as we all know, fully blessed by records of extraordinary friendships:

Loving brotherhoods, as affectionate & replete-with-depth, as that of Damon & Pythias, & Castor & Pollux; & also, to my overworked & overwrought & possibly even totally frazzled mind right now, come Androcles & The Lion, The Three Musketeers, & The Town Mouse & The Country Mouse;
& There are obviously sisterhoods still more powerful, & more noble, than those evoked by Sappho, upon the isle of Lesbos...

—Friendships based on mind, on soul, on heart, & (yes, indeed!) on spirit

—So that when I myself hear of various transparently opportunistic, purely functional, merely provisional & short-sighted, & generally vulgar & altogether wholly debasing definitions of that otherwise lovely word "Friendship," such as those which I have described above, get all choked-up—in the specific sense of, such definitions make me want to run to the nearest wailing wall I can find & immediately throw open one of the windows I hope to locate there & (yes—& yuk) just *barf*!

*

However, fortunately, it would seem that often public opinion, too, can see through, & thus duly detests
False "Friendships" representing merely some cutely convenient, manifestly careerist idea of "Mutuality";
—"Friendships" reflecting, at best, mere *conflicts-of-interest*.

—C.f., for example, in relatively recent, if not actually latter-day American history:

Those of President L. Johnson & his pals in the military, vis-à-vis the misinformation they gave out, re the scandals & atrocities which, for their part, they committed or collaborated on, in Vietnam—& which his assistants stopped keeping secret it seemed, the very second Johnson died;
The "Friendships" of one-time U.S. President R. Nixon & those of his frantically bean-spilling, so-called "Loyal," predictably & appropriately betraying, one-time Watergate "Friends";

The "Friendships" of President R. Reagan vis-à-vis his secret deals re Iran-
Contra, etc., conducted beneath tables overturned in the end at the
drop of a top-hat;
Or even those of President G. Bush, with one of his own sons (no less),
involved in scandals related to various fouled-up, failing, yet firmly
U.S. government-backed, domestic savings-&-loans banks

—& So I speak out here against

"Friendship" that's provisional, & fleeting, & which will not stand the test of
time (& often, not even casual examination, much less any really
serious stress at all); & which will not stand the test of *distance*, either,
once any such mis-defined "Friend's" back is turned about (not to
mention when one's own back is turned about, even for just one
instant)

—Which I myself have found, happens almost always
(Again & again, oddly enough, it happens almost always)
Happens for almost all of us, I've noticed, *at the absolutely worst possible
moment*

—Which is, for all of time, & for all of space, & for even *life itself*, whenever
& wherever

All the chips are going down . . .

OF "THE TAGANKA TROUPE" IN SOVIET RUSSIA, 1957

For Yuri Lyubimov

Today, ever-changing, incorrigibly erratic, struggling young "Federated
Russia"! But, practically only yesterday, that staid old Soviet Union!
For seventy long years under the Soviets, winter & summertime too,
icy stronghold of that dull old Socialist Realism!

—& Yet, circa 1957, following the death, in 1956, of Soviet dictator Joseph
Stalin, during a brief period of so-called "Thaw"
"Escaping The Commissars!" (as the enthusiastic article dated 1967, from
The New York Times "Sunday Entertainment Section," excitedly,
unfolding fresh as a daisy, again reminds me)
The brave, the bold, the dazzling jazzy, the critically-acclaimed upstart
"Taganka Troupe"
Performed for a couple of precedent-shattering evenings, to top off leaden-
footed, official Moscow meetings

—Introducing, to its conservative, astonished, & ominously frowning
audiences
Of much bemedalled generals clad in full-dress uniforms, bewhiskered
government officials sporting baggy, pin-striped tuxedos,
bespectacled collective-farm deputies garbed in spotless work-clothes,
& other such dubious representatives of "The People"
Sketches incorporating, of all things, nothing less than Western,
"decadent," Avant-Garde style, cabaret theater!

—Daringly, bursting the bonds of the usual, dancing unconcernedly in the
very midst of the obvious,
Spangled men in black top-hats & tights, strutting girls in white top-hats,
glistening white silk shorts, & highly polished, high-heeled, patent-
leather shoes
All carrying black, plastic, capitalistic, rhinestone-studded canes, like
"Hoofers" straight from Broadway added a note of risk—& poetry—

To what started out as the usual series of so-called "Serious," so-called
"High-Level," Soviet-style, domestic-problems-type discussions, over
groaning after-dinner banquet-tables,
Regarding only "Kilowatt Hours," regarding only "Tractot-Quotas"...

Oh brave (&—as soon became clear—also foolhardy) Taganka Troupe!
Officially censured, critically-forsaken & fallen-out-of-favor, locked up
only a few months later, in the 1957-model Soviet refrigerator
To play Chekhov, & *minor* Chekhov only, before various indifferent
collective-farm families, huddled in huts in the lower Ukraine,
You disappeared from the world—even the world of theater—suddenly &
almost totally
Like faithless love, like yesterday's newspapers—*The New York Times*, alas,
not excluded—

To get quietly lost, like so many other really exceptional things, in the trash-
can of ordinary, everyday human history
—That "History" with only scant follow-up; that history, sometimes,
without even *any* memory...

—So that suddenly, only a couple of decades later, during politically highly
"Conservative" & so-called "New Conservative" times here in our own
land
Instead of reading, for example, enthusiastic praise of theatrical
phenomena like you, Taganka Troupe, & your sassy, outrageous,
indomitable spirit, in such politically attuned, influential places as, for
example, *The N.Y. Times* "Sunday Entertainment Section," & also
elsewhere
What we had to read, all too often, all during the 1980s, & continuing for a
while even into the 1990s—regarding theater, the visual arts,
literature generally, & sometimes even poetry—
Were all those straight-faced, esthetically recidivist, generally tedious & chic-
ly "New Conservative" articles & reviews, replete with critical sermons
& tirades
On "The Avant-Garde Betrayal," & on "The Death Of Modernism," & on
"Post-Modernism & Its Rise"

—So that it may have seemed to some readers of those commentaries that it
was all a mistake, yes, perhaps all just one great big mistake,
You, brave Taganka Troupe!—&, while our own bear-footed, trend-copying,
anti-intellectually trigger-happy, politically-influenced national
cultural commissars were at it,
The entire revolutionary, experimental, American 1960s as well, starting
with its beginnings was—or so they seemed to suggest—all a bust &
one great big regrettable error!

. . . Oh brave (& daring) Taganka Troupe! Like a natural part of our inmost
hearts beating throughout recorded history, but nonetheless, every
now & then, suddenly declared somehow "superannuated"
You drift, still, in & out of my memory—whether or not perfectly
remembered; you live by impulse in the main, instead of by
name . . . like a lock of hair
That turns up, years later, in an anonymous Valentine
From a sender whose name was once well-remembered; you stand
suspended, almost in mid-air, crazy as a frontiersman's rifle hung on a
wall in some suburban living-room, or a bar in some otherwise dreary,
work-a-day, American "Levittown" . . . a sign of lost life . . .

Still, I continue to dream of you! & with love, I think of those brilliantly
spangled, outrageously radiant, resplendently shining, dancing
Men, each brazen gesture soon, so soon, apparently trapped forever by the
Soviet chill, & also their government-issue greatcoats; & I think of
those women, once so resplendent in their white top-hats & their silk
shorts, & also declared so soon, so superannuatedly "Scandalous"
—& I think above all of the leader of that troupe in his top-hat, leading all
the rest, with his rhinestone-studded cane, who dared to tell them all
there once, & also all of us, for all time (or at least for as long as we
ourselves are still truly free to listen)

That bravest, most daring & sometimes hardly imaginable thing:

To wit: that our own lives could be (couldn't they be?)

Just a little bit more amusing.

(1987–1996)

OF AN ONLY CHILD'S WORLD

1.

It's hard for anyone who hasn't grown up as an only child to imagine just
exactly what that's like, I guess,
However (& I think I can speak with a certain authority about this subject,
having grown up, once, as an only child)
I believe that, just as with most other things in this world (if not, in fact, just
as with just about everything else on earth)

In understanding this particular subject, too,
A little stretch of the imagination can help.

2.

I'll bet that you, for example—right off the bat & even just for openers—can
imagine quite easily
That "Only," can sometimes mean kind of "Lonely"

—I mean, after all, for *any* only child, right from the start,
There are no elder sisters, & no elder brothers, nearby, much less in the very
same room
For a kid to talk to when it gets dark, or cry out in the night to;
Therefore, a child who is an only child, will often fall asleep at night

Listening to TV, or to the radio.

3.

Nor is there any big sister, or big brother to turn to, daytimes, to give the
only child the benefit of his or her experience,
By offering the usual advice, on things like "How To Get Along In Life;"

On the other hand, there can be a certain element of excitement, can there
not?—& even a certain "Pioneering Sense of Exploration" (as we
might term it, to be brief)

In "Finding Out Things For Oneself."

4.

Of course, in such a situation, it's also true, there's no little sister, or little
brother either
To watch over, look out for, share various favorite toys with, & perhaps,
sooner or later, to become jealous of;

—Yes, I can say from experience; & even with a certain authority,
That it's inconceivable, for an only child, to experience anything at all

Like the usual feelings of "Sibling Rivalry."

5.

In any event, a kid can get to be kind of independent,
Growing up that way, relatively-speaking on his or her own; & all by his or
her own lonesome;
He or she learns to look "Within," in the main, for solutions to many of the
usual, youthful "Growing Pains,"
—First during childhood, & then in later years;

Revolving his or her own thoughts, & racking his or her own brains again &
again, about various things that, to be sure, concern other people, too.

—Such as what, in the world, might be best for one.

6.

—Even the parents one might have depended on a whole lot more (&, yes,
maybe even loved a whole lot better), had not one, from early on,
started the habit of "Going It Alone,"
Being seen—whether those two were sleeping invisibly together, during the
long dark hours of the night, in the room they inevitably gravitated to,
which was their private space,
Or whether they were hard at work, during long hours of the daylight, &
thus also absent & in some other place—

As presences in a world of *their* own, too; & always merely "Out There
Somewhere," somewhat like mysteries;

—& What with all the preoccupations of their own, adult, lives

As distant as stars or galaxies.

7.

—The fact that in their own younger years, *they* were once accompanied,
Being testified to, by seemingly endless hosts
Of laughing-&-joking-together aunts & uncles, etc., passing through the
    halls many nights—& passing by one's bedroom door, & into radiant,
    multicolored party-lights;
& Coming & going, during their frequent, mysterious visitations,

Like meteors or like comets.

8.

So, just possibly, it takes a certain peculiar kind of courage for a kid to go on
    growing up that way—as isolated, & separated, & aware of the
    vastness & indifference of the darkness that surrounds him or her
As our astronomers are, scanning the universe, from all around the world,
    with their optical & radio telescopes;

All hoping—amid the obscure, unanswered silences that they know, too—

To hear one signal or find just one sign
That our earth is not the only inhabited planet in the universe.

FROM OF GARTER BELTS; & ALSO OF THE HOOKS & SNAPS ATTACHED TO THE GARTER-STRAPS CUSTOMARILY DANGLING DOWN THEREFROM

1.

Sometimes I wonder: is there anybody in the world who realizes how
amazing, ingenious, yet truly functional (even though seemingly
merely a highly decorative, charming thing)
A garter-belt—not to mention the various garter-straps, & hooks & snaps of
the four garter-straps
Customarily attached to it, & hanging down from it, really is?

Yes, like most of the truly worthwhile things in this world—i.e., like science,
like arts, & indeed all forms of beauty, & even like making love itself
It, too, has its wonders—partly in proportion to its inventiveness, its
cleverness, &—in relation to the cunningly-fashioned, wondrously
exquisite female shape which it will embrace, usually,

Its absolutely necessary complexity!

—Why, it's really an incredible contraption, a garter-belt is, designed of
course (some might say) "simply" to firmly hold up a woman's two
delicate, indeed often gossamer-like stockings up
—But in actuality, featuring an intricacy of design which is tremendous!

For example, speaking for myself, every time I chance to encounter on the
highways, the byways, or even the bedrooms of this great land
A woman standing around in front of me & wearing a garter-belt, —
waistband; four straps—& at the bottom of each—two matching sets
of hooks & snaps

I must confess that I'm overwhelmed by an emotion not unakin
To what I experience when beholding a sketch for a scientific invention, or
some drawing for a gigantic fabrication or fortification by Leonardo
da Vinci

Or some other great & nobly devoted inventor
Of (mainly) bones for poor suffering humanity.

—Yes, the garter-belt reminds me, for one,
Of things like the magical complexity of Orville Wright's first bi-plane
Which fused a motorcycle engine with paper-thin wings
So as to hold up an entire apparatus, somehow, virtually in mid-air.

Bi-plane?—I dunno, perhaps tri-plane would be more like it.

2.
Therefore, let us look further into the wonders of the garter-belt,

—Beginning, of course, with the waistband, that slips around many a lady's charming, & even, as the picturesque descriptive saying goes, "hour-glass" waist
So elastic, that a lady may feel that she is embraced.

Itself, that waistband, a little marvel of appropriate, yet delightful invention—located well above the garters themselves, to be sure, yet still attractively well-placed
Cunningly, between the torso & the hips, where even the average femininely-formed lady is already, to my eyes—
Even if she is not my own amour; in fact, even if she is hostile to me, & is wearing a suit of armor—
Is so strikingly, & often dramatically curvesome, in formation
(Nor let us forget the role of the discretely ingenious, tiny, tightening hook-&-eye hook at her back,
—& Concluding our considerations, of course, with the elastic garter-straps
Of which [God Save The Mark], there are usually four, as you know, unless you've been lately dropped from some other planet, attached to any garter belt, sewn on tightly at the top
&, At the bottom, which are affixed to the stockings held up so tightly
By means of various rubber tabs, & metal [or, sometimes] plastic) clips

—Which latter structure is perhaps, the heart of, the key to the entire
apparatus; & to which we shall turn our attentions in greater detail
later

—The same kind of apparatus which is, to be sure, customarily attached to
other "unmentionables" which we should also—at least in passing
certainly at least mention here
I.e., which one will also find attached to any properly well-made,
appropriately-constructed teddy, basque, mini-basque, braselette,
bustier, waist-cincher, or corselette or even (yuk!) corset;

—Unless, of course, one has come loose somehow; or fallen off.

3.
Sometimes, of course, garter-straps are detachable;
That is to say, removable, on a whim.
& That is surely why, on some disappointing occasions every now & then
A gentleman may look steadfastly at a lady wearing one of those charming
garments which, standardly,
Should be replete with the garter-straps
Customarily attached to any properly well-made, appropriately-constructed
teddy, basque, mini-basque, braselette, bustier, waist-cincher, or
corselette or even (yuk!) corset;

& Search & search in vain, all around, for them, & think them carelessly lost
or missing
When in fact they may simply have been removed
—Perhaps left inside a dresser-drawer, or even thrown off into a corner, all-
too-hastily & hurriedly (I at least think);

& (Yes I'd even say) quite carelessly!
Simply so as not to get in the way.

4.
& that is generally a mistake, I think, too; & yet one more misguided attempt
(as happens already far too often in this all-too-often all-too-tedious,
uninspired, & solely practical world of ours)

Yes, one more misguided attempt, to substitute for our visual delight, &
sense of the appropriately decorative generally
Some relatively conventional, & relatively commonplace sense of
functionality, & uninspired, uninspiring /so-called "practicality"

Yes!—as if a lovely, already astonishingly lovely, curving, & invitingly-
shaped waist, thighs, & (come to think of it) tummy, did somehow
not deserve to be ornamentally
Framed, still further, in its contours, for the admiring viewer & especially for
the would-be wooer, for the admiring "viewer & woo-er" (as the saying
goes, which I myself have just invented)
Just like some pretty picture!—&, what's more
As if even the loveliest of ladies' legs were only best when revealed starkly; &
plainly; & barely; & what's more
As if even the loveliest of ladies' legs on earth were only meant
For stomping back & forth to the grocery-store
Or to prevent the bottom of her torso from falling onto the ground or
floor—

[. . .]

9.

Yes, it is this little device, the garter, with all its hooks & snaps, & which is
designed so wisely, cleverly, ingeniously, & architecturally to
maximally beautiful effect,
Which renders stockings for almost any lady—as far as I'm concerned, & as
far as I can see,
At present as well as in the future, something that will never let her down

Yes, & even though it's true, that it is based on sound principles
physiologically, technologically according to the laws of physics, &
medicine, & good health

The garter-belt might seem to some, sometimes, perhaps occasionally a
little bit rather inconvenient to put on, & attach,

(Especially for example if the lady is in a rush & late)

No garter-belt much less garter is surely half as inconvenient for the woman
who dons stockings, & who puts them on, one-by-one, & then
properly affixes them
As it was inconvenient for the designer who designed it to create:

—Probably some diligent, female-admiring yet somehow also self-
sacrificing person
Taking some well-deserved time off
From designing things for all humanity: like computer terminals,
equipment for airplane control-towers, cables for cable TV
companies, plumbing & electrical supplies; toilets or perfumes for
toilettes; or even, spare parts for typewriters & tugboats.

RITA & RINGO

for Rita Tushingham & Ringo Starr

1.
It's obviously dangerous in poetry, if you want your poems to last,
To risk making reference after reference
That just might not make much sense

To readers, just a few years later. After all, isn't it difficult enough for a poet
to write poems which have a chance to last for a long time, anyhow
Without stacking the deck against himself or herself that way, in the here &
now?

2.
Such risky—since alas potentially senseless—references, it's clear,
Would include allusions to various half-forgotten, bygone times, & relatively
unknown places
& Similarly interesting things, unfamiliar to even most informed people
today;

—On the other hand, there are also references not too far-flung but perhaps
too familiar to consider
Such as much contemporary slang & other such probably temporary,
potentially obscure nomenclatures,
Which might seem strange as Sanskrit to readers, by even the very near
future

—& Perhaps chief among the latter, are most references to individual
people such as pop-stars, popular at any given moment.

3.
Let's make a little leap then, into just the recent historical past
& Look at the problems, re making references to a couple of individuals I
can think of
Which—if we'd been writing poetry involving them just a few decades
ago—we'd now face:

For example, let's pretend that we're writing in the year 1963 A.D.; & that somehow you or I have suddenly perceived something of significance—or, at least, that we think is significant—about two top pop-stars
& That we'd like very urgently to "Communicate To Eternity" . . .

—Say, for example, we suddenly perceived back there in '63 that:

Rita Tushingham, the charmingly winsome actress starring in the then-brand-new British film *A Taste of Honey* (then just making her debut as rising star, thanks to her stirring portrayal of a runaway girl befriended by a sensitive homosexual)
& Ringo Starr, the charmingly winsome, brand new drummer for the British rock-&-roll group The Beatles (then just making his debut as rising star, too, thanks to both his stirring drumming in tunes like the Beatles's first 45 RPM single "Love Me Do," & also his somewhat startling hairdo)—
Both of whom, that year at least, displayed rather whimsically off-beat, & (I for one think) curiously endearing, quasi-"Unisex" faces—

Share a certain, rather striking, physical resemblance.

& Let's pretend, too, that the reason why we're absolutely convinced that the resemblance of those two talented stars is significant,
Is because we've come to believe that the quasi-"Unisex" look we think they share
Foretells nothing less than the much-forecasted & long overdue, final (truly final)

DECLINE & FALL OF THE ENTIRE BRITISH COLONIAL EMPIRE!

—What with the traditional emphasis of that formerly vast global enterprise on distinctly masculine values & all
When, for prior century after century, it dominated practically the whole wide world
& Was most conventionally "Successful."

4.

Let us suppose then that, following our sudden realizations & quasi-epiphanies, madly inspired
With our eyes rolling around wildly, our tongue hanging out & our hair standing up on end despite the breeze,
One of us rushes to our clattery, old-fashioned, pre-computer-era typewriter,
To make at least a temporary little household racket, by writing a poem about all that;

Since, happily & deservingly, charmingly winsome Ringo is still quite well-known both as singer & actor,
But the equally charmingly winsome Rita has already, alas & double alas, even as I write this—despite other, later & stellar, stirring performances in such major films as *Doctor Zhivago* (1965)—been mostly & unjustly forgotten today
Instead of having contributed an interesting insight on 20th century World History back in '63, as we expected,
Wouldn't we then—if we'd referred only casually & without much further explanation to her (but not to him) in our creation—

Have been practically dooming our poem to oblivion?

5.

Possibly. But since the majority of any poet's works will of course, alas (& double-alas!), probably be totally forgotten anyway,
Among others which he or she has higher hopes for (those poems, for example, intended to last at least as long as King Tut's tomb)

Let this poem too, praising the continuing stardom of Ringo Starr but deploring among other things the fall from popular favor of that fine actress, Rita Tushingham
Risk being mistaken by some, for a "Throwaway Poem"—

Such as a writer will sometimes whimsically produce, designed specifically for the light amusement of himself or herself & perhaps a few old friends . . .

"YOUR LIFE IS YOUR OWN LIFE . . .": VARIATIONS ON A THEME BY JAMES WRIGHT

1.
Your life is your own life & not just a compendium of debts;

No, never just a mosaic of owings, whether real or imagined
—A life like the latter would be no life, surely, but only an excuse for not
    living, & for existing as if continuously inside someone else's skin;

Nor can anyone develop "A Life Of One's Own" in the opposite way, I think,
    & by looking at the world with eyes merely of creditor, or predator,
—I.e., like someone who thinks that the balance of the world is out there
    just simply to owe him or her a living

For our lives are surely our own lives, are they not;
—& Not just a compendium of debts.

2.
Some day I'd like to understand why even the very idea of the existence of
    individuals so bold or foolhardy as to attempt to think & live
    independently
& Who have therefore only themselves to blame if something happens to go
    wrong,
Should alarm so many people & even scare some almost half to death.

—Apparently producing in the average mind, quasi- apocalyptic visions of
    the whole world falling apart, with the heavens falling down & seas
    rising up; & with volcanoes erupting underfoot with every step;
With entire governments collapsing & institutions crumbling; &—still
    worse yet!—with even such leading members of the community at
    large
As bankers & brokers & accountants
Throwing clawing, despairing hands up to the heavens, as if revenues might
    yet be found there

As con-men & parasites of all kinds, having bitten their fingernails to the bone & torn out all their hair, climb out onto lofty window-ledges & prepare to end it all,
By throwing themselves as hard as possible onto the smoking ground

—While churchbells around the world toll out ominously, to warn the faithful of impending doom.

3.

However, show most regimented people some really sleazy, two-bit miserable weasel
Whose external life consists solely of various semi-balletic attempts to keep in step, toe the mark, or somehow fall back in line,
& Whose so-called personal life is a crazy-quilt woven of casual, highly unreliable, or forced & fraying connections
& Whose inner life is either virtually non-existent—or else some miserably shabby collection of endless, self-perpetuated ruses as to his or her own unique worth

& It's then that people start nodding & smiling to themselves as if understandingly—& suddenly start to show some real respect.

4.

It's refreshing, I find, to speak every now & then with people ready to take responsibility for their own actions,
I.e., People who are really genuinely present, even as they're standing there right in front of you.
& Whose existences aren't merely contingent upon ruses or excuses as they go through life, struggling daily under the shadow of endlessly-evoked mysterious, frightful injunctions or secret, invisible, awful obligations,

I.e., People who aren't either suffering from the dread disease of too much noblesse oblige or else, just plain helpless, hungry, or hard up.

5.

—Not that I think that I myself have achieved so exquisitely liberated a state, despite my frequent, indeed constant efforts. Still, sometime at least,

I'd just love to encounter a whole playful day's-worth of people fit for
freedom at least by temperament
& Who since they've gained relatively firm control over their own lives
Can refuse flat out to make excuses for the lives they're living

—If only just to provide a welcome sense of relief, at least briefly, from the
way things too often are; & if only as a form of experiment.

OF LIVING ALONE BUT NOT BROODING TOO MUCH ABOUT IT

To live alone is to be immensely in charge of the silence
So that, if you have something to think about, you will probably think about that something long & hard; & probably—since you're usually able to—uninterruptedly, too,
Possibly for entire afternoons or evenings, or indeed for whole days on end.

Therefore, if you are living alone &—*horrors!*—are therefore mostly by yourself, with only yourself to keep yourself company (except, of course, for an occasional visitor)
It's especially important, I think, to accomplish things especially wisely & well, since—just in case you foul up on things—you're the only one you're probably going to be able to blame for things that happen to go wrong.

Certainly, if you are living alone, it's important to choose those friends & acquaintances, & lovers, too, whom you do see, especially wisely & well
—That is, for their benign & unannoying qualities,
Lest they endlessly crowd your mind, & cloud the horizon of your thoughtfulness, by giving you pointlessly troubling things to think about,
Such as problems they themselves may have refused to solve, or may have been unable to solve, in relation to their own lives,

—Possessing, as most people do, the scattering distractions of, say, a busily uproarious, merry family; or of highly sociable room-mates coming & going like cuckoos popping in & out of cuckoo-clocks;
Or, even, of multiple beeper-units which they have had installed upon their telephones, so as to prevent them—should they ever happen to be alone, & receive, for example, a thought-provoking phone-call—
From having to follow any single thought straight through to its natural end.

In-dwelling groups know almost nothing about privacy.

—For there, there is always, inevitably, some erratically interruptive,
intrusive bit of bullshit going down
Which, minimally, renders the possibility of "Continuity Of Thought"—
much less consideration of the mental well-being of those people
living alone, & who may, therefore, be highly disposed to treasuring
"Continuity Of Thought"—
Highly unlikely; & any serious perspective of sensitivity, vis-à-vis the
situation of a person living alone—& thus with only himself or
herself to blame for things that happen to go either right or wrong—
In general, almost impossible!

—But persons living alone should not think too much about all this
But rather substitute for many such defensive, negative thoughts as those,

The idea, above all, of choosing friends wisely & well
From among those people, for example, who have been responsible for
themselves, & for themselves alone, for at least some few moments, &
for at least some continuous time

Within recent memory.

Afterword

TIME

The cleft in my hat
                          is bearing a little soot
A seed falls
A few fanning spears
Of grass
            are there
And now a red flower